Implicit Bias in Schools

Implicit bias is often recognized as one of the reasons for instances of discrimination and injustice, despite most people explicitly believing in the importance of equality and justice for all people. *Implicit Bias in Schools* provides practitioners with an understanding of implicit bias and how to address it from start to finish: what it is, how it is a problem, and how we can fix it. Grounded in an accessible summary of research on bias and inequity in schools, this book bridges the research-to-practice gap by exploring how implicit bias affects students and what school leaders can do to mitigate the effects of bias in their schools. Covering issues of discipline, instruction, academic achievement, mindfulness, data collection, and culturally relevant practices, and full of rich examples and strategies, *Implicit Bias in Schools* is a must-have resource for educators today.

Supplemental material, including links to resources mentioned in the text, tools, and worksheets to assist your journey when implementing strategies at your own school can be found at www.routledge.com/9781138497061.

Gina Laura Gullo is Educational Equity and Data Consultant at GLG Consulting and Adjunct Professor at Lehigh University, USA.

Kelly Capatosto is Senior Research Associate at the Kirwan Institute for the Study of Race and Ethnicity at Ohio State University, USA.

Cheryl Staats is an education author and researcher with a background in implicit racial/ethnic bias.

Other Eye On Education Books Available from Routledge
(www.routledge.com/eyeoneducation)

Implicit Bias in Schools

A Practitioner's Guide

Gina Laura Gullo, Kelly Capatosto, and Cheryl Staats

Routledge
Taylor & Francis Group

NEW YORK AND LONDON

First published 2019
by Routledge
52 Vanderbilt Avenue, New York, NY 10017

and by Routledge
2 Park Square, Milton Park, Abingdon, Oxon, OX14 4RN

Routledge is an imprint of the Taylor & Francis Group, an informa business

© 2019 Taylor & Francis

Library of Congress Cataloging-in-Publication Data
A catalog record for this title has been requested

ISBN: 978-1-138-49698-9 (hbk)
ISBN: 978-1-138-49706-1 (pbk)
ISBN: 978-1-351-01990-3 (ebk)

Typeset in Optima
by Out of House Publishing

Visit the eResources: https://www.routledge.com/9781138497061

To all those experiencing implicit bias everyday

May this book be one step in the journey that will end discrimination.

Contents

Meet the Authors

Gina Laura Gullo, Ed.D.
GLG Consulting; Lehigh University

Gina Laura Gullo is an Educational Equity and Data Consultant at GLG Consulting and an adjunct professor at Lehigh University. Gina's research interests focus on unintentional bias in K-12 schools and communities. Her current work investigates how administrators' implicit bias affects school discipline decisions and on the barriers to the superintendency experienced by female educational leaders. With a doctorate in educational leadership and a master's in special education from Lehigh University, in addition to a bachelor's in psychology from The College of New Jersey, Gina pursues efforts that help to bridge the educational research-to-practice gap with a driving goal to facilitate the proliferation of evidence-based practices for equity in modern schools. She values community and professional service, within which she advocates for equity and inclusion for all people through data use and education.

Kelly Capatosto M.A./M.P.A.
Kirwan Institute for the Study of Race and Ethnicity at Ohio State University

Kelly Capatosto is a Senior Research Associate at the Kirwan Institute for the Study of Race and Ethnicity at Ohio State University. Kelly leads the Institute's work on implicit bias, and she co-authors the annual report, the *State of the Science: Implicit Bias Review*. Her research focuses on equitable policies and decision-making in the fields of education, juvenile justice, and child welfare. Kelly is a three-time OSU graduate with a bachelor's in psychology and a master's in both school psychology and public administration.

Cheryl Staats, M.A.

Cheryl Staats has an extensive research background in implicit racial/ethnic bias. For five years, she was lead author of the Kirwan Institute's *State of the Science: Implicit Bias Review*, an annual publication that synthesizes scholarly literature on how unconscious racial associations influence human decision-making and outcomes. Cheryl earned a Bachelor of Arts degree in Sociology and Spanish from the University of Dayton, and a Master of Arts degree in Sociology from The Ohio State University.

Preface

The need for social justice in our world continues to be met with exciting research and strategies to help build more inclusive and equitable communities. However, in the midst of our own busy careers and daily demands, it's impossible to translate every last bit of this research into something meaningful and practical for our lives.

Our Story

The three of us came together around this same need: to make the research relatable to real people who can use these insights to have the greatest impact on their communities. Specifically, we wanted to focus on bringing one topic to light: implicit bias. This term has been a "hot topic" in the news and social media. Implicit bias is often recognized as one of the reasons for the ever-present instances of discrimination and injustice, despite most people explicitly believing in the importance of equality and justice for all people. We wanted to help unpack this disconnect between our intentions and values and what ends up happening through our behaviors and interactions. When we fail to consider and challenge our implicit bias, we all play a role in maintaining this "disconnect" on a societal level.

In our efforts, we also acknowledged the importance of integrating an institutional lens alongside the conversation of interpersonal bias. Such a consideration is of paramount importance for our public education system because the U.S. has a longstanding political and legal focus on promoting equity that often fails to be actualized in the day-to-day school environment.

By integrating this systemic lens across the landscape of implicit bias, we are able to uplift strategies to not only celebrate diversity, but to challenge a legacy of historic inequities.

A Systems-Changing Challenge

In many ways, this book was an opportunity for us to challenge ourselves to do this systems-changing work in practice, and we wanted to be intentional about having difficult conversations and naming things at face value. We aimed to do this by highlighting instances where we all have been negatively impacted by bias while simultaneously leveraging our privilege to speak to and challenge persistent inequities that have long-plagued communities of Color – particularly Black, Latinx, and New American communities. You may notice that we capitalize the "C" in of Color throughout our text. This is one such way we recognize the shared inequities and individualized cultures of the peoples represented in this term.

Many have suggested that, "ally is a verb," meaning that the goal of pursuing equity work from an ally-ship perspective is active in nature. Allies not only recognize privilege but strategically leverage their privilege to advance opportunities for others who are not given the same benefit of the doubt – whether due to racism, sexism, ableism, etc. Thus we continuously challenged ourselves to make this book a way that utilized our privilege to advance equity in school and uplift the ideas and experiences of those most impacted by implicit bias.

Lived Experiences of Bias

As this book is primarily about implicit racial bias, we wanted to make sure we were *practicing what we preached* while also keeping each other accountable and checking our own biases – especially to ensure that this work did not speak *on behalf of* any community. We are mindful that silencing the lived experiences of others under the guise of ally-ship and/or research rigor is a tremendous threat to equity work everywhere. Thus, while we all heavily rely on our academic and professional experience, we do not consider ourselves as "experts" on the personal and community-level experiences of racial marginalization and oppression.

You will see shared lived experiences of bias in boxed text throughout this tome that offers stories of both implicit discrimination and perspectives to help fuel the changes needed to promote real equity and inclusivity in today's world. We hope that these narratives will help to humanize issues related to implicit bias. While people who are on the receiving end of bias are experts in their individual, lived experiences, the "validating" research often takes years to follow. As researchers in our profession, we openly acknowledge this disconnect between experience and empirical validation, and hope that this combination of research and experience can help bridge this divide in a way that will encourage our education system toward real change to promote equity and inclusion efforts through an implicit bias-conscious lens.

We, as authors, must also acknowledge that social identities are too often portrayed as a monolith: meaning our personal experiences with bias and its effects can vary greatly across identities and circumstances. For example, the experiences of bias based on race, religious affiliation, gender, sexuality, and immigrant status manifest in very different ways. However, by challenging bias for any person, we aim to lay the groundwork that will dismantle the expression of bias toward every person.

The Writing Journey

In our writing journey, we felt a similar interplay between our understanding and personal experiences with bias stemming from our own individual identities. On the one hand we are writing this book from a place of privilege, but we are also writing this because we have all experienced bias in real and challenging ways. It's often difficult to write on a topic like this when we all have a very personal stake in the game; however, we view such experience as an asset.

We lead this text with our own stories and identities to establish the foundation for why this work means far more to us than it might on a purely conceptual level.

"Who Are *You* to Be Talking to *Me* About Race?"

When I (Gina Gullo) brought my dissertation topic to my advisor, I was asked this very important question. I hold this question central to all of my research to this day. If I can't tell you why you should listen to me or why I should be studying something, then I'm not doing the right thing. Dr. Floyd Beachum, my doctoral advisor and mentor, helped me to understand that studying race was not about trying to change the world but about human beings. He challenged me, and challenges me still, to think about the world with not only a critical lens but also an understanding, perspective-taking, and privilege-cognizant lens. In writing this book, we all found ourselves approaching this question in different ways and with different tools. Sometimes our answers were that we were not the people best to write the book but rather the people who *were* writing it; and so, we've included the voices of as many of those who have the real stories to tell as possible. Other times, we found ourselves working as communicators facing a world where practitioners and researchers traditionally only idealized the idea of "bridging the research-to-practice gap." We are three women, three writers, three people all passionate about understanding implicit bias and giving educators the tools to remedy the effects of implicit bias – sometimes that must be enough.

Who Is Gina?

I am a White, married, middle-class, mother. I identify best as female, but if you talk to me about the continuum of gender, sexual orientation, and romantic orientation you will get a far more complicated answer. I grew up at or below the poverty line with divorced parents (and a stepmom), three brothers (and a deceased sister), and in a very White neighborhood for most of my childhood. I have a bachelor's in psychology, master's work in behavioral neuroscience, a master's degree in special education, and a doctorate in educational leadership. None of this makes me the right person to tell you about implicit bias.

At a professional development program I was helping to run, a video was played that showed Black parents talking about the fear they live with for their children's safety. One story was about how the kids could not be playing with water guns and another about removing hoodies from a son's wardrobe. Pregnant at the time, the video brought me to subtle tears. While I would never have to fear for things like this, I needed to raise a son who wouldn't perpetuate such parenting needs. Instead of fearing for my son's safety, I face concerns about building a world around him that doesn't instill implicit bias – it's not really possible. How could I bring another White, upper middle-class male into this world knowing that it would be so easy for him to become another part of the problem? The answer lies in the privilege.

As a White person, I'm often terrified to admit I'm privileged and still have that go-to instinct to say, "well I didn't do anything to get it," or, "but I don't want it." I know those are not legitimate responses and stop myself now, yet they are still my natural, implicit responses. During my time researching and learning more about race and implicit bias, I've started to reconceptualize my privilege as a tool. I don't believe that equity will ever completely exist, and consider my privilege as a pedestal that lets other people hear a message. When I write about race, I'm not given the "angry Black lady" response or the "entitled immigrant" scoff. I still get the "pretty good for a woman" reaction from time to time, but when I talk to someone about implicit bias they are ready to hear about the possibility of them being racist by accident because "it's natural." So many are terrified of being called racists, or any kind of -ism supporter. With my White lady smile and small stature and voice, I am privileged in the perfect way to help people accept implicit bias not only in the world, but in themselves. It may not be "right," but this how I use what socially just practices I can offer to use my voice in promoting equity as much as possible.

– Gina Laura Gullo

Who Is Kelly?

The topic of implicit bias is something incredibly meaningful for my personal journey and passion for equity. I come to this conversation from a unique perspective. I am someone who benefits from White privilege, and people rarely make assumptions about my character or competence based on my race or ethnicity.

I am also Latina, and although I have never experienced any discrimination on the basis of my own identity, I have witnessed and learned of many instances where the people I love most have encountered bias in many forms. Oftentimes, that bias was difficult to identify. It could manifest as something subtle like pointing out how hard a name was to pronounce. Sometimes it was easier to identify, like making fun of an accent. In any case, I usually believed this behavior was typically not intended to cause anyone harm.

For a long time, I found it difficult to reconcile how people that valued equality could still make such hurtful comments. Learning about implicit bias was an important piece of the puzzle. It helped me understand how bias, even if unintended or unconscious, can still have a real impact on others. This research also taught me how important it is to learn about my own bias, reflect on how my behavior may be impacting others, and speak out when I see someone experiencing bias – even when it's awkward or could reflect poorly on me. Writing this book has been a very important step in using my privilege to shed a light on bias and create more equitable and inclusive school environments.

The education system is one of the most important institutions in our society. What we teach our youth and the opportunities we provide them will determine the values and success of our society far into the future. I am so excited to have the opportunity to share information about implicit bias with people who can have the biggest impact on students by challenging its impact.

– *Kelly Capatosto*

Who Is Cheryl?

As my colleagues have already acknowledged, grappling with the privileges of our respective identities was a consistent task that undergirded our efforts in this book. This was not only a means of personal introspection, but also an ongoing dialogue in which we openly held each other accountable. While some imperfections of this nature may persist in these pages, we collectively sought to do justice to this research, uplift the voices of those most affected by implicit biases, and bring a practical, action-oriented spirit to the final product, all while also remaining true to our own identities and life experiences.

Like many others, I come to this work from a path that I didn't realize I was walking until I was reasonably far along. I never set out with the intention of researching implicit bias. Perhaps the most concise summary would say that a series of happenstances and fortunate timing, coupled with my fascination for understanding people, brought me into this realm. The further I delved, though, the more enthralled I grew. The notion that people act on their unconscious association, and the idea that these associations can interfere with even the most well-intended individuals' ability to successfully realize their intentions for equity, is tremendously powerful yet is in no way a valid excuse for the persistence of explicit biases and the harmful outcomes thereof.

My own story of the challenges and biases I have faced pales in comparison to many others, and while comparison in this area isn't fruitful (after all, no one "wins" when it comes to suffering oppression), these experiences nevertheless shape who I am. While I may never fully understand the experiences of those dissimilar to me, I offer one of my most prevalent character traits: the persistent desire to listen. I don't just mean listen to hear; I mean listen to understand. It is my hope that when you read the stories of implicit bias experiences that people have generously offered us to include in this book, you use these stories not as a means of comparing plights, but rather as an opportunity to understand another's story. I believe listening with a spirit of understanding can be a tremendously profound way of moving toward justice in the world.

– *Cheryl Staats*

Who Are You, to Be Listening to Us Talk About Implicit Bias?

We approach this book with a school leader audience in mind. While much of the writing in this book focuses on school principals and assistant/vice principals as school leaders, we hope that this book is equally as meaningful to central office staff, superintendents, and teacher leaders. You, as an educational leader, should be able to learn more about implicit bias overall and how to work to counteract the effects of implicit bias in your school and/or district by reading this book. Perhaps you are still studying to become a school leader in a principal or superintendent certification program: We hope this book will provide you the tools to work toward equity and inclusivity from your first day of internship until the day you retire, but caution that this is an unending learning process. For the experienced leader or the leader-trainer reading: We hope that your depth of knowledge and experience is complemented and heightened by your reading of this book. Understanding that as a school leader your time is preciously limited, we offer now a bit more about how you can read this book and use its special features.

How to Read This Book

This book is presented in four parts to help guide your reading experience. Part I provides an introduction to bias (implicit and explicit) including a legislative and research history, different presentations of bias, where biases come from, and measurement of implicit bias. If you are already very familiar with implicit bias you may choose to skip this part of the book and go directly to Part II of the tome. In Part II, we discuss how implicit bias impacts students both in academics and discipline. Here you will learn more specifically about how and in what ways implicit bias affect students. In Part III, we provide strategies for reducing the effects of implicit bias in schools in two chapters: one focused on individual and one focused on institutional methods. We begin with individual strategies in the spirit of "being the change" and "walking the talk" so that leaders like you can not only focus on leadership for implicit bias remediation, but also provide a walking example of how that looks. We end the book with three very different invited author chapters in Part IV of the book. Each case approaches implicit bias in schools with a different first-hand perspective, with the first helping you see the policy development process and gather ideas about how to frame your own policies, the second providing you with information on how to develop a professional development seminar on implicit bias that meets the needs of your specific school, and the third offering you a better understanding of the lived experience and challenges associated with this work. You may choose to begin the book with Part IV to create a context for understanding implicit bias in schools through the eyes of those working through these changes or you might read through the book from start to finish. We encourage you to read the book in the order that makes the most sense to you – in a diverse world of school leaders your experiences with implicit bias will be different than the next leader: choose your own reading adventure.

Special Features

In addition to the various parts of this book, you will find some boxed text in the book that is intended to provide additional information to supplement your reading. These additions may provide interesting facts, potential resources, or even a higher level of detail on various aspects of the book. Similarly, we present tables and figures in the book to provide supporting information to the text that is often presented in a more visual-learner-friendly manner. You will find even more supplemental material on the book website, including links to some of the resources mentioned in the text as well as tools and worksheets to assist your journey when implementing the strategies described at your own schools. Finally, we have included short personal accounts of bias throughout the book from real people working and learning in schools. While we, as authors, can describe the research to you, we do not have the experiences with bias that many live through daily. We include these self-told stories to embrace as many voices as possible: if you have a story to include you can email the authors at implicitbiasbook@gmail.com to add to our online collection of lived experiences. When you read, use the supplemental items to support your experience while you support the learning experiences of those around you. Talking about bias (and reading about bias) will not be easy, but stick with us and we will leave you with the tools to *DO*.

eResources

Additional resources for download can be found by visiting the book product page at https://www.routledge.com/9781138497061. Once there, click on the tab that reads "eResources" and then select the file(s) you need, which will download directly to your computer.

Contributors

Invited Chapter Authors

Kimberly Brazwell, M.Ed.
KiMISTRY LLC; KLFS Corp
Kimberly Brazwell is a social justice advocate and trained facilitator with experience in designing highly interactive, trauma-informed workshops through the practice of mindfulness and storytelling. Passionate service has opened doors for Brazwell as a highly requested speaker and dialogue facilitator with invitations ranging from training workshops in the States to keynotes as far as Germany. Brazwell has over 15 years of experience in educational administration, diversity and inclusion efforts, wellness advocacy, and community building. She is an alum of Ohio University with a Bachelor of Science in Interpersonal Communication and a graduate of Ohio State University with a Master's degree in Educational Policy and Leadership. KiMISTRY, Brazwell's consulting firm, specializes in reshaping the "fit" perspective by examining the intersectionality of equity and inclusion, behavioral healthcare, and holistic wellness for a trauma-informed experiential application to human engagement. In 2017, she published a memoir on workplace trauma entitled *Browning Pleasantville*. Outside of consulting and writing, Brazwell is a community advocate, executive director of the King Lincoln Family Services Corporation, artist, trained facilitator, visual practitioner, and blessed mother of two daughters.

Pamela A. Fenning, Ph.D., ABPP
Loyola University Chicago
Dr. Pamela A. Fenning is a Professor of School Psychology at Loyola University Chicago School of Education and served as the director of the

Doctoral School Psychology Program from 2001–2015. She was a principal investigator on an evaluation study of multi-tiered behavior support in six large high schools. Her research and clinical interests focus on multi-tiered academic and behavioral interventions, equity and evidence-supported practices in school discipline, interdisciplinary collaboration, and competency training in school psychology. She has published widely in the area of school discipline and equity in school-based behavioral practices. She is the chair of the National Association of School Psychologists (NASP) Professional Positions Committee. Dr. Fenning holds a Ph.D. in School Psychology from the University of Wisconsin-Madison. She is a licensed clinical and school psychologist in Illinois.

Miranda B. Johnson, J.D./M.P.A.
Loyola University Chicago
Miranda B. Johnson is a Clinical Professor of Law at Loyola University Chicago School of Law and the director of Loyola's Education Law and Policy Institute. She teaches experiential learning classes in education law and supervises law students in the representation of parents and students in school discipline and special education cases. She has also presented in various settings on prevention-oriented approaches to school discipline and organized training programs for school administrators on school discipline issues. Prior to working at Loyola, she was a staff attorney at Advocates for Children of New York, an organization promoting access to better educational services for New York City school children. She holds a J.D. from New York University School of Law and a Master in Public Affairs from Princeton University's Woodrow Wilson School of Public and International Affairs. Before law school, she taught social studies at a residential high school in Colorado and conducted research in Tanzania on a Fulbright Scholarship.

Kimberly Barsamian Kahn, Ph.D.
Portland State University
Dr. Kimberly Barsamian Kahn is an Associate Professor of Social Psychology at Portland State University and leads the Gender, Race, and Sexual Prejudice (GRASP) research lab. She received her Ph.D. in Social Psychology from the University of California, Los Angeles and completed a postdoctoral fellowship at Lisbon University Institute in Portugal.

Dr. Kahn's research addresses contemporary forms of implicit bias and subtle prejudice from both the targets' and perceivers' perspectives. She has conducted empirical research and interventions to reduce implicit bias and stereotyping within education systems, work organizations, and police departments. Her work has been funded by the National Science Foundation, the Society for the Psychological Study of Social Issues, the Bureau of Justice Assistance, and the National Institute for Transportation and Communities.

Lived Experience Contributors

Note: Affiliations and roles in quotations reflect those during the lived experience shared in this book. Current roles and affiliations may differ.

Anna Danylyuk
"Charter School Teacher, Philadelphia, PA"

Donna Druery
Research Associate & Project Coordinator, Texas A&M University
"Predominantly White Institution Student"

Rachel Roegman
Assistant Professor, University of Illinois, Urbana-Champaign
"Graduate Student, New York, NY"

Brandon Wallace
Faculty Associate, Johns Hopkins University; Lecturer, Montgomery College (Germantown); Adjunct Professor, Prince George's Community College
"Teacher, Baltimore City, MD"

Donte Wood-Spikes
Youth Activist & Artist, Columbus, OH
"K-12 Student in Predominantly Black and Predominantly White Schools"

What Is Implicit Bias?

Implicit What?

Knowing Isn't Everything

Have you ever made coffee in the morning on "autopilot" or drove to school without trying to remember how to get there? What about choosing what to have for lunch: how often do you really think about all of the options available? You don't need to know what you are doing to get things done. You can tie your shoes without making bunny ears and read a book without sounding out each word. All of these thought processes are implicit, or unconscious. How did you decide to read this book (and if you have to read it for class or professional development, then why right now)? Perhaps you chose it from a list of books on implicit bias or saw a review you liked. Maybe you were assigned this book and realized that you had to read it now or you wouldn't get the reading done in time. These kinds of thoughts are more explicit, or conscious. Implicit thoughts are those we don't really think about and just do, while explicit ones are those where we consider options and often reason our way to conclusions.

This book is dedicated to the part of our cognition that is activated involuntarily and outside of our intentional control. By definition, implicit bias refers to stereotypes and attitudes that occur unconsciously and may or may not reflect our actual attitudes. Although unconscious, implicit biases can affect our perceptions, actions, and our decisions across realms ranging from the relatively trivial (e.g., recognizing that "green means go" on a stoplight) to those quite significant (e.g., in a school discipline situation, which student is perceived to be more or less culpable than another). This chapter begins the conversation to understand how – regardless of our explicit intentions – the unconscious part of our cognition can shape our actions and ultimately the outcomes that occur in educational environments.

Good Intentions Gone Wrong

On Halloween, Muslim students were allowed to "opt out" of the Halloween parade and festivities if they felt it would violate their Islamic beliefs. This turned into a huge disaster! Muslim students were sent to an "exclusion room," where I was supposed to supervise. The room was not set up for us, and there were not enough supplies for all the children. Even worse, other teachers began to see the Muslim student room as a "punishment room" and began sending misbehaving students there from every grade. Eventually there were over 60 students in the room, with no space for them to even sit. The Muslim students were left alone and appeared miserable. Stuck for hours in the "punishment room," the students were unable to complete any activities and surrounded by disgruntled older students sent to the room by teachers who saw the Muslim activities as a punishment rather than an accommodation. I told my grade-team lead, who reported the incident to administration. Even though I received an apology, the students still have not.

– Anna Danylyuk

Education for ALL

The desire for our education system to support every student along the pathway to success is embodied by the United States Department of Education's mission to "promote student achievement and preparation for global competitiveness by fostering educational excellence and ensuring equal access" (U.S. Department of Education, 2011, p. 1). Schools need to equip all students – regardless of race, ethnicity, gender, or ability status – with the opportunities and skills necessary to

The U.S. Department of Education claims to work toward this mission in two ways: by the secretary and department leading national dialogues on result improvement and by the administration of a variety of education-focused programs.

reach their full potential. Despite these good intentions, achieving these aims is challenged by issues rooted in the educational system such as overworked teachers, extensive standardized testing, and paperwork that seems to never end. In addition to these pressures, person-to-person issues such as language barriers, children who have experienced trauma, and differences in cultural backgrounds may impede educators' progress in developing relationships with their students. Outside of schools, even more factors can contribute to students' success – family support, economic advantages, neighborhood dynamics – this list can go on and on. Taken together, schools are facing an uphill battle in the pursuit of equitable academic excellence access.

If we want to make schools a place that benefits *all* students, we must explore why our intention to provide educational opportunities falls short of producing equitable outcomes.

A critical piece of this puzzle is the immense need to highlight the importance of students' identities as a factor that can support or inhibit their academic and social-emotional development. A growing body of research on implicit bias (also called unconscious bias) demonstrates that aspects of an individual's identity such as race, gender, or ability status are associated with a variety of stereotypes that can influence how others perceive or interact with that individual.

Don't Sound the Alarms Yet!

While bias typically holds a negative connotation, bias is in actuality a neutral term. You might have a bias for summery weather or delicious food as opposed to an ice storm or sour milk. Not all biases are harmful and in some cases they can be quite helpful. Next time you avoid stepping on a wad of chewing gum, know your bias for clean ground is there to assist you.

Biased perceptions can unintentionally influence decision-making and actions outside of conscious awareness in ways that do not mirror our explicit commitment to equality (Greenwald et al., 2002; Kawakami & Miura, 2014). Often, these biases reflect stereotypes and patterns of marginalization in society rather than what we actually believe or feel. In acknowledging that implicit biases often run counter to the values that we – as educational leaders – hold, we begin to understand the nuances of how inequities can persist in the absence of overt discrimination. By revealing the nature and operation of implicit bias, the authors of this book hope to move readers toward becoming better practitioners, leaders, and people.

What Is at Stake?

Our nation's students depend on schools to uphold their commitment to educational excellence and equal access. When we fail to uphold this commitment to all students we encounter issues like the **achievement gap** between White and racial minority students – particularly Black and Latino students as compared with White students. While the achievement gap as a whole has narrowed in the past 50 years, notable progress has stalled. According to National Assessment of Educational Progress (NAEP) data, the progress made to begin closing the achievement gap in the 1970s and 1980s reached a plateau by the early 1990s, since when it has remained relatively stable (Barton & Coley, 2010). Figure 1.1 shows the achievement gap since the early 1990s. Beyond the academic outcomes, racial disparities occur along the pathway to achievement including different levels of advanced course access for Black and Latino students as compared with White and Asian students (who have far greater access) – especially for math and science (Office for Civil Rights, 2016).

> The **achievement gap** refers to differences in the academic results (test scores, higher education, job attainment) between different groups of students – typically between students who are Black and students who are White. Similar terms include the *opportunity gap*, which refers to differences in resources and educational quality, the *learning gap* referring to differences between what students actually learn and what they are expected to learn, and the *discipline gap* referring to differences in how often students of different groups are suspended and expelled from schools. In all of these gaps, low socioeconomic status students and students of Color typically experience more detrimental outcomes (lower test scores, more suspensions) than White students.

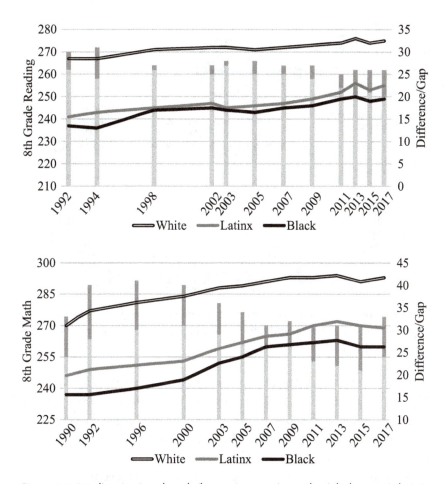

Figure 1.1 Reading (top) and math (bottom) scores in grade eight by race/ethnicity are shown as lines with the Black–White gap shown as the dark gray bars set behind the smaller Latinx–White gap shown with the light gray bar. Only years with available data are shown

(NAEP, 2018)

Academic achievement is only one, albeit large, piece of this puzzle. Punitive discipline use can limit students' educational opportunities and even push students toward justice-system involvement – otherwise known as the school-to-prison pipeline, as illustrated in Figure 1.2. As Senator Dick Durbin (2012) described in an address to Congress on the school-to-prison pipeline, "For many young people, our schools are increasingly a gateway to the criminal justice system. What is especially concerning

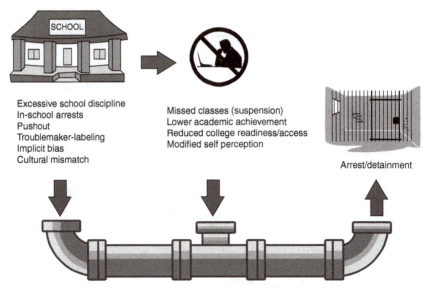

Figure 1.2 The school-to-prison-pipeline represented graphically here is how many think about the contribution of school practices to future involvement in the criminal justice system

about this phenomenon is that it deprives our children of their fundamental right to an education" (p. 1). By calling attention to the culture of punitive discipline prevalent in public schools, Senator Durbin urged the committee representatives to consider the implications of school discipline practices and the role of race in disciplinary outcomes.

Researchers often explore links between the achievement gap and the discipline gap, considering that these gaps might be "two sides of the same coin" (Gregory, Skiba, & Noguera, 2010). Just as expected, disparities in school discipline are just as pronounced and pervasive as academic disparities (American Civil Liberties Union, 2008; Losen, Hodson, Keith, Morrison, & Belway, 2015; Office for Civil Rights, 2016). For example, the Office of Civil Rights' analysis of 2013–2014 discipline data found Black students were 3.8 times more likely to receive an out-of-school suspension than White students (Office for Civil Rights, 2016). The data also revealed American Natives, Latinx, Pacific Islanders, and multiracial boys were disproportionately suspended, but to a lesser extent than Black boys. Other studies show drastic differences in days suspended by race for students with special needs, with Black students with disabilities receiving three times as many days of lost instruction as White students with disabilities

(Losen, 2018). These examples are just small pieces of part of a large body of evidence showing disparities in school discipline that span across racial, gender, and ability identities. Together, these disparities in academic and discipline outcomes contribute to persistent racial differences in high school completion rates (Barton & Coley, 2010; Reeves, Rodrigue, & Kneebone, 2016).

As these disparities show, we still need to address the inequity in our education system. Before we provide you with the knowledge and tools you need to begin this process through implicit bias remediation, we must begin by considering the influence of our collective past. By examining the education system's policies, practices, and historic barriers to achieving racial equity, we can better understand how implicit biases emerge and learn from previous successes and failures to improve educational trajectories for students of Color. Like other national institutions, the education system is part of a legacy of legally endorsed discrimination. Though a full retelling of this history is outside of the scope of this book, it is worth considering key points in our history that made a lasting imprint on the course of public education. Let's begin our story with a brief history of relevant research, practices, and policies that best represent the interplay between racial equity, social science, and K-12 education.

A Brief History of the Intersection of Race, Social Science, and the Education System

Largely considered the first time that social science research played a major role in advancing racial equity in public education, the work of Kenneth and Mamie Clark had a large impact on the end of segregation in public schools. The Clarks' body of work, often referred to as "The Doll Studies," explored the effects of racial segregation on Black youth's self-esteem and development (see Clark & Clark, 1939, 1947). These experiments showed that Black boys and girls overwhelmingly attributed a variety of positive attributes (e.g., pretty, nice) to a White doll, but attributed negative characteristics to a Black doll – despite knowing they more closely resembled the Black doll. The Clarks summarized the findings from their doll studies in a 1950s report to the Mid-Century White House Conference on Children and Youth to help build a case that living in segregated communities and going to segregated schools left a lasting negative imprint on Black youths' social-emotional and educational development (Library of Congress, 2012). Most importantly, this report was cited as evidence in favor of desegregation in the landmark case: *Brown vs. Board of Education of Topeka*. Following the victory of Brown, and the subsequent passing of the Civil Rights Act of 1964, other researchers in education and the social sciences followed in the Clarks' footsteps to better understand the effect of integration in schools and to help educators meet their legal obligations of providing equal education opportunities regardless of race. Shortly after the passing of the Civil Rights Act, the Elementary and Secondary Education Act (ESEA) was enacted in 1965 (U.S. Department of Education, 2016). The goal of ESEA was to affirm the national commitment to equal opportunity for all students by establishing Title I federal aid to support this effort. ESEA also added specific provisions to addressing poverty and discrimination for Indigenous populations, including Native Hawaiian and Alaska Native students (U.S. Department of Education, 2016). These overarching federal policies enacted during the 1960s led educational professionals to find innovative ways to ensure they were supporting their students, regardless of race.

A simple YouTube video shows various recreations of The Doll Test where students of Color repeatedly make similar statements to students in the original 1940 experiment. The original experiment was dramatized in the 1991 film, *Separate But Equal*, starring Sidney Poitier as Thurgood Marshall.

One of the most historic examples of a practitioner-led effort to grapple with the experience of privilege and prejudice was the "blue eyes-brown eyes" exercise conducted by Jane Elliot and rumored to occur on the day following the assassination of Dr. Martin Luther King Jr. in 1964. (Peters & Cobb, 1985). In her third grade classroom, Elliot provided explicit privileges to students with one eye color and explicitly marginalized students with another eye color. This imposed power dynamic affected every dimension of how the classroom activities were structured (e.g., who was allowed to sit next to whom, who could speak, etc.) and even played out within the students' relationships. Her controversial exercise offered an unfiltered perspective of how racial discrimination operated and paved the way for teaching professionals to begin to explore both the explicit and subtle manifestations of racism and power in a school setting.

> *Eye of the Storm* is a 1970 documentary by ABC News and Xerox Films that details Jane Elliot's experiment. It can be viewed free of charge at: https://archive.org/details/EyeOfTheStorm_201303

As one of the first empirical, or scientific, studies to address how teachers' beliefs impacted student outcomes, Rosenthal and Jacobson (1968) examined how teachers' expectations related to changes in students' academic ability. Ostensibly, the researchers tested children to assess their academic potential, labeling only some students as soon to "bloom" (Rosenthal & Jacobson, 1968, p. 19). The classroom teachers were led to believe that this group of students would achieve more in the upcoming year than the rest of the class – even though there were no actual differences between these two groups. At the end of the school year, all students participated in the same test of general ability (TOGA) as was originally given to the students. "Ready-to-Bloom" students had more pronounced gains from the original test than their peers.. Although contemporary researchers have highlighted some of the limitations present in the original study, this work elevated the concept of the "self-fulfilling prophecy" in educational discourse (Rosenthal & Jacobson, 1968, p. 20).

Following the progress seen after the 1960s civil rights legislation, the 1970s continued the momentum through federal-level efforts to support other marginalized student populations as depicted in Figure 1.3. Of great significance were amendments issued to Section 504 of the Rehabilitation Act of 1973, which eliminated discrimination on the basis of ability status in public education institutions (Wegner, 1984). Additionally, the 1970s and 1980s saw great progress in a narrowing of the achievement gap between Black and White students (Barton & Coley, 2010).

Rather than focusing on legislation directed toward marginalized student groups, the 1980s saw shifts in the governance of public education funding, with much authority diverted from the federal government to the states. For example, the Education Consolidation and Improvement Act (ECIA) implemented in 1981 greatly reduced the role of the federal

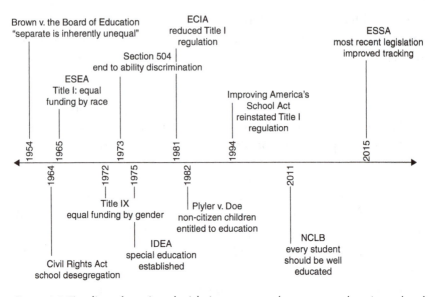

Figure 1.3 Timeline featuring legislation most relevant to education-related civil rights

government in regulating Title I (Darling-Hammond, & Marks, 1983). This era marked a long period of absence for federally endorsed policies that specifically addressed racial equity issues in education. Although the Improving America's Schools Act of 1994 re-asserted the role of federal government in supporting marginalized students through Title I funding, the United States would not see another large-scale federal effort to specifically address disparities between White and minority students until the reauthorization of ESEA in 2001 (U.S. Department of Education, 1995, 2016).

As federal investment slowed, higher education institutions began to fill this gap in addressing racial inequities in K-12 education through theory and practice. During this time, academic scholarship on educational outcomes for racial minorities and other marginalized students abounded. Although it is beyond the scope of this book to provide examples that encompass this vast range of empirical literature, much of the work in this era explored the social and environmental sources that contributed to racial disparities in education and identified ways to improve pedagogical practices to support a diverse classroom. Some of the foundational bodies of work on cultural competence and multicultural education established in the 1980s are shown in Table 1.1.

Table 1.1 Foundations of Cultural Competence and Multicultural Education in the 1980s

Year	Author(s)	Topic
1939	Clark and Clark	The Doll Study
1964	Elliot	Blue Eyes–Brown Eyes Study
1968	Rosenthal and Jacobson	Self-fulfilling prophecy – "bloom" study
1980	Au	Culturally Appropriate Instruction
1986	Bennett	Data-Based Decision-Making Structure
1986	Gollnick and Chinn	Multicultural Education – Microcultures
1987	Erickson	Culturally Relevant Pedagogy
1987	Sleeter and Grant	Taxonomy of Multicultural Education

By the 1990s, early progress in closing the achievement gap, or discrepancy between the academic success of Black and White students, slowed to a halt (Barton & Coley, 2010). Shifts in public attitudes and the political climate eventually built momentum toward implementing standards-based educational reform at the federal level. The goal was to provide more oversight and accountability in the process of ensuring all students reached academic proficiency. Eventually, this shift resulted in another reauthorization of the ESEA, better known as No Child Left Behind (NCLB, 2001).

Under NCLB, the federal government worked with states to develop proficiency standards that were tied to Title I funding with the goal of incentivizing academic excellence with a re-ignited focus on improving outcomes for marginalized students. As such, NCLB legislation required schools to implement standardized testing practices to ensure that students from third to eighth grade were reaching proficiency in math and reading (U.S. Department of Education, 2004). Additionally, schools had to document whether certain subgroups of students, which included racial minorities, English Learners (ELs), and students in special education, were reaching the same standards.

Although this was ostensibly a move in the right direction for holding schools accountable for ensuring racially equitable achievement outcomes, its implementation has often been criticized for being overly punitive and actually broadening gaps (Shepard, Hannaway, & Baker, 2009). To illustrate, if a school did not make "adequate yearly progress" (AYP) by failing to reach its state's proficiency goals and closing achievement gaps, the school was penalized with a variety of sanctions, including losing Title I funding and the possibility of a state takeover or even school closing

(NCLB, 2001, p. 1446). Many critics of this policy argue that instead of supporting marginalized students, NCLB created a vicious feedback loop where schools would lose the very supports they needed to improve equity and academic achievement (Darling-Hammond, 2007; Fusarelli, 2004). As such, many viewed this policy as a detriment to the goal of closing educational gaps rather than a solution.

Addressing many of these criticisms, ESEA was reauthorized in 2015 with the Every Student Succeeds Act (ESSA), which remains the current legislation (U.S. Department of Education, 2016). Among other benefits, preschool development grants provide funding opportunities targeted toward neighborhoods where racial minorities, ELs, and those living under the poverty line are often represented. States can choose their own indicators of success beyond standardized test scores. If desired, states can opt to identify school climate, closing the achievement gap, or decreasing discipline disparities as their goal – offering a unique avenue for addressing racial inequity in public education. Although ESSA shows promise toward mitigating existing racial disparities, the impact of these changes are not yet realized.

As evidenced by this long and often troubling racial history in education, we still have a long way to go in addressing negative outcomes for students of Color, particularly Black and Latinx youth. However, it is also worth acknowledging the vast amount of progress made toward addressing the interpersonal and psychological dynamics between teaching professionals and students, and their contribution to racially disparate outcomes. Emerging from early work on cultural competency, multiculturalism – the consideration of one's openly held beliefs, values, and expectations – has provided the backdrop to help educational professionals address the influence of known, conscious aspects of their social identity. This progress helped set the stage for our current need to address the impact of implicit bias, which – unlike explicit bias – occurs unconsciously and without intent (Greenwald & Krieger, 2006).

Setting the Stage for the Next Steps: Considering Implicit Bias

Today, the following question emerges: how can policies and programs designed to promote equality have such minimal impact over time? Shedding light on this matter, implicit bias research can help you, as an educational leader, understand how the best intentions to improve equity can be interrupted and never reach the desired outcome of improving students' trajectories. This interplay between history, policies, and processes that perpetuate longstanding inequity is deeply connected to the ways implicit bias can influence actions and decisions in current educational practices – especially since these structures can contribute to the formation and manifestation of our collective implicit biases.

Given the long history of racial disparities in educational outcomes, educational professionals, policymakers, and advocates are compelled to explore all of the factors that may contribute to these adverse consequences. Until recently, the effect of implicit bias was a proverbial stone left unturned. Fortunately, by using the lens of understanding our social cognition, we can shed new light on why these disparities occur. Additionally, insights from implicit bias research can help inform how educational institutions and actors can intervene and move forward in developing support practices that benefit all students.

As such, the goal of this book is to apply this foundational body of research on implicit bias and education to your real-world practice. In Part I, we guide you in an exploration of what implicit bias is, how it differs from other forms of bias, and how we can measure it. Part II summarizes for you the latest knowledge on the effects of implicit bias on PreK-12 students, followed by Part III which provides you with evidenced implicit bias remediation strategies. In Part IV, we connect the research to your practice with a series of three invited author chapters where educational professionals are putting implicit bias remediation into action. It is our hope that by illuminating these examples, you will not only be equipped but also inspired to address implicit bias in your school as a critical step toward educational equity.

References

American Civil Liberties Union. (2008). *School to prison pipeline: Fact sheet.* Retrieved from www.aclu.org/racial-justice/school-prison-pipeline-fact-sheet-pdf

Barton, P. E., & Coley, R. J. (2010). *The black-white achievement gap: When progress stopped.* Princeton, NJ: Educational Testing Service. Retrieved from www.ets.org/Media/Research/pdf/PICBWGAP.pdf

Civil Rights Data Collection (CRDC). (2016). *2013–2014 civil rights data collection: A first look*. Retrieved from www2.ed.gov/about/offices/list/ocr/docs/2013-14-first-look.pdf

Clark, K. B., & Clark, M. P. (1939). The development of consciousness of self and the emergence of racial identification in Negro preschool children. *Journal of Social Psychology, 10*, 591–599.

Clark, K. B., & Clark, M. P. (1947). Racial identification and preference in Negro children. In T. M. Newcomb & E. L. Hartley (Eds.), *Readings in social psychology* (pp. 169–178). New York, NY: Holt, Rinehart & Winston.

Darling-Hammond, L. (2007). Race, inequality and educational accountability: The irony of No Child Left Behind. *Race Ethnicity and Education, 10*(3), 245–260.

Darling-Hammond, L., & Marks, E. L. (1983). *The new federalism in education: State responses to the 1981 Education Consolidation and Improvement Act*. Santa Monica, CA: RAND Corporation. Retrieved from www.rand.org/pubs/reports/R3008.html

Durbin, D. (2012). *Ending the school-to-prison pipeline* [transcript]. Retrieved from www.judiciary.senate.gov/imo/media/doc/12-12-12 DurbinStatement.pdf

Fusarelli, L. D. (2004). The potential impact of the No Child Left Behind Act on equity and diversity in American education. *Educational Policy, 18*(1), 71–94.

Greenwald, A. G., & Krieger, L. H. (2006). Implicit bias: Scientific foundations. *California Law Review, 94*(4), 945–968.

Greenwald, A. G., Rudman, L. A., Nosek, B. A., Banaji, M. R., Farnham, S. D., & Mellot, D. S. (2002). A unified theory of implicit attitudes, stereotypes, self-esteem and self-concept. *Psychological Review, 109*(1), 3–25.

Gregory, A., Skiba, R. J., & Noguera, P. A. (2010). The achievement gap and the discipline gap: Two sides of the same coin. *Educational Researcher, 39*(1), 59–68.

Kawakami, N., & Miura, E. (2014). Effects of self-control resources on the interplay between implicit and explicit attitude processes in the subliminal mere exposure paradigm. *International Journal of Psychological Studies, 6*(2), 98–106.

Library of Congress. (2012). *Kenneth Bancroft Clark papers: A finding aid to the collection in the Library of Congress*. Washington, DC: Manuscript Division. Retrieved from http://rs5.loc.gov/service/mss/eadxmlmss/eadpdfmss/1998/ms998002.pdf

Losen, D. (2018, Apr 14). *Racial discipline disparities among students with disabilities: Research findings and implications for state and local action*. Session presented at American Educational Researcher Association Annual Conference: New York, NY.

Losen, D. J., Hodson, C. L., Keith, I. I., Morrison, M., & Belway, S. (2015). *Are we closing the school discipline gap? K-12 racial disparities in school discipline*. UCLA: The Center for Civil Rights Remedies. Retrieved from https://civilrightsproject.ucla.edu/resources/projects/center-for-civil-rights-remedies/school-to-prison-folder/federal-reports/are-we-closing-the-school-discipline-gap/AreWeClosingThe SchoolDisciplineGap_FINAL221.pdf

National Assessment of Educational Progress (NAEP). (2018). NAEP Data Explorer [dataset]. Retrieved from www.nationsreportcard.gov/ndecore/xplore/NDE

No Child Left Behind Act of 2001, P.L. 107–110, 20 U.S.C. § 6319 (2001).

Peters, W. (Director, Writer), & Cobb, C. (Writer). (1985, Mar 6). A class divided [Television series episode]. In W. Peters (Producer), *Frontline*. Boston, MA: WBGH Education Foundation.

Reeves, R., Rodrigue, E., & Kneebone, E. (2016, Apr). *Five evils: Multidimensional poverty and race in America*. Washington, DC: The Brookings Institute. Retrieved from www.brookings.edu/wp-content/uploads/2016/06/ReevesKneeboneRodrigue_MultidimensionalPoverty_FullPaper.pdf

Rosenthal, R., & Jacobson, L. (1968). Pygmalion in the classroom. *The Urban Review, 3*(1), 16–20.

Shepard, L., Hannaway, J., & Baker, E. (2009). *Standards, assessments, and accountability: Education policy white paper*. Washington, DC: National Academy of Education. Retrieved from http://files.eric.ed.gov/fulltext/ED531138.pdf

U.S. Department of Education. (1995, Sept). *Archived information: The Improving America's Schools Act of 1994*. Retrieved from www2.ed.gov/offices/OESE/archives/legislation/ESEA/brochure/iasa-bro.html

U.S. Department of Education. (2004). *A guide to No Child Left Behind.* Washington, DC: Office of the Secretary, Office of Public Affairs. Retrieved from www2.ed.gov/nclb/overview/intro/guide/guide.pdf

U.S. Department of Education. (2011). Mission. Retrieved from https://ed.gov/about/overview/mission/mission.html

U.S. Department of Education. (2016). *Elementary and Secondary Education Act of 1965: As amended through P.L. 114–95, enacted December 10, 2015.* Retrieved from www2.ed.gov/documents/essa-act-of-1965.pdf.

Wegner, J. W. (1984). The antodiscrimination model reconsidered: Ensuring equal opportunity without respect to handicap under Section 504 of the Rehabilitation Act of 1973. *Cornell Law Review, 69*(3), 401–516.

2 | Forces, Sources, and Discourses of Implicit Bias

Introduction

In the last chapter we discussed how the goals of our educational system are threatened by the risks associated with bias, and explored how the legislative and research history has helped prepare schools to meet this challenge. Recall that implicit bias is *the stereotypes and attitudes that occur unconsciously and may or may not reflect our actual attitudes.* While our explicit bias – or actual attitudes – seem to drive our decisions, often we actually make decisions using our implicit biases instead. In this chapter, we focus on the functions of implicit bias, where this bias comes from, and how we can measure implicit bias in an effort to better understand and discuss it.

Blame It on Your Brain!

The roots of implicit bias lie in evolutionary patterns. If you see two mushrooms and have to eat one, would you pick a beige or bright pink mushroom? You don't really know anything about the mushrooms, but in a forced-choice situation you make a guess based on your past mushroom experiences and what you already know. We stereotype foods, clothing, neighborhoods, cell phones, news channels, politicians, even beverages (juice looks healthy...). Many times making decisions based on categorization doesn't amount to much more than a more efficient decision-making process, but when categorization leads us to discriminate and harm we need to address it. When we need to make a decision with little or no information, when our decisions need to occur quickly, when we don't have the energy to focus on making a decision: that's when we are forced to resort to implicit bias. It's the bare-bone, efficient decision-making force that gets you an answer without really thinking about the answer.

And Now for the Complicated Version...

According to Dr. Neuroscientist, you begin by detecting a response conflict between your goals/external cues and automatic biases (Stanley, Phelps, & Banaji, 2008), proceed to evaluate the situational context in your medial prefrontal cortex (Molenberghs & Morrison, 2014), and subsequently use your dorsal-lateral prefrontal cortex to combine the data and make a decision about how to behave (Cristofori et al., 2016). Furthermore, the inferior frontal gyrus activates on one side when stereotypes are considered and on the opposite side when one alters a response to a stimulus in a way that supports or challenges the stored stereotype data (Mitchell, Ames, Jenkins, & Banaji, 2009).

While you may not want to make decisions or act based on implicit bias, your brain might have other plans. Your brain is all about efficiency: humans often navigate our world by filling in the logical gaps rather than having the full picture. Even your eyes don't take the time to see everything; your occipital lobe generates much of what you see based on what it already knows about the rest of the image (see Farah, 2000). When it comes to making decisions, your brain only uses some of the information available as well. Let's try a research-based activity, the Stroop Task (Stroop, 1935). Look at the words in the list in Figure 2.1 on the next page. Read them as quickly as possible, saying out loud the color of each word rather than the actual text. Can you do it in less than five seconds? OK, go!

In the Stroop Task your brain wants to read the text, but you are using several areas of your lateral prefrontal cortex (the part that you use to tell yourself what to do) to tell your brain to name colors instead (Botvinick, Cohen, & Carter, 2004). When working to overcome implicit biases, your brain is challenged in a very similar way. Making the choice

BLACK

GRAY

WHITE

GRAY

WHITE

BLACK

BLACK

GRAY

BLACK

GRAY

WHITE

WHITE

BLACK

GRAY

WHITE

GRAY

BLACK

Figure 2.1 This is a monochrome version of the Stroop Task. Read the color names
(not the text) from top to bottom as quickly as you can without pausing

to avoid decisions made on "autopilot" requires you to realize your autopilot is not the same as your desired behavior and then actually choose to consciously make the decision. Pair that with the stress of 30-plus students in a 45-minute (if you're lucky) class period, and you can begin to see how the difficulty grows. The process gets even more complicated when you realize you have a part of your brain that is half involved in storing stereotypes and half involved in changing your behaviors based on those stereotypes. The take-home message is that acting in ways that don't match over-generalizations adds some stress to the brain. The more cognitive load (stress on your brain functioning), the more likely bias will cloud your decisions – and we have only talked about the front part of your brain so far!

When we think about the brain as a whole, we start to see a distinction between implicit and explicit processing in the time it takes for your brain to respond to different items. Implicit bias reactions occur more quickly than explicit bias reactions to the extent that they are discernible in the brain as different responses (Derks, Stedehouder, & Ito, 2015; Healy, Boran, & Smeaton, 2015; Hehman, Volpert, & Simons, 2014; Williams & Themanson, 2011). In fact, your brain takes almost twice as long to react explicitly as compared with implicitly – although the difference is only about 200 milliseconds. Your brain wants to jump to conclusions to keep you functioning as quickly as possible (Hinton, 2017), but sometimes your brain gets the wrong information leading to poor choices. Fortunately, if you continue to practice making a better decision, you can override the "autopilot" response of your brain more easily (Amodio, 2014). Try to read the list a few more times and notice that the task gets easier: practice even makes perfect when retraining your implicit biases.

Who Told My Brain That All X People Are Y?!

As educators, we understand the continual learning that takes place from birth to one's final breaths. Consider the phenomenon of "environmental text" that works to teach beginning word knowledge to young students through exposure to common text like the names of food chains or popular department stores. As children enter kindergarten, they have an idea of what a word is – even if their parents never had the opportunity to show them a book – through exposure to environmental text. No one provided any formal exposure or instruction to these students, but they come to school with a basic knowledge of words and letters. Biases are formed in very much the same way – especially implicit biases (Rudman, 2004a, 2004b).

If you try to stay abreast of current events, you must access the news in some form. One way implicit biases form is by internalizing the way that information is covered through the media (Rudman, 2004a). Consider the two headlines below:

Implicit bias can cloud perceptions such as culpability versus innocence. Implicit bias that favors White individuals has been linked to more frequent perceptions of anger on Black versus White faces (Hugenberg & Bodenhausen, 2003), higher perceptions of aggression when students moved in "traditionally African American" manners (Neal, McCray, Webb-Johnson, & Bridgest, 2003), and an increased likelihood to favor policies where juveniles were sentenced as adults (Pickett & Chiricos, 2012). While individually these perceptual differences may seem small, when conflated they can lead to the criminalization of individuals regardless of actual behavior.

KILLER FACES CHARGES IN CIVIL SERVANT MURDER SUSPECT FACES CHARGES IN POSTAL WORKER DEATH

These headlines are for the same story and offer the same denotation but substantially different connotations. Labeling bias often labels individuals with negative terms such as criminal or negligent as opposed to more neutral terms such as suspect or forgetful (Allen, 2015; Baker, 1994). Bias through labeling can be heightened through use of positive or negative spin as shown in these headlines:

IMMIGRANTS TAKING MORE U.S. JOBS NEW CITIZEN UNEMPLOYMENT DECLINES

As you continue to take in the news, more drivers of implicit and explicit biases come into play: bias by omission (not reporting contrary details), bias by expert selection (talking to experts more likely to support certain views), bias by commission (using inaccurate facts to support assumptions, possibly unknowingly), bias by story selection (only reporting on certain kinds of events), bias by placement (putting preferred news at the top/front), and countless variants. Media bias doesn't stop with the news; it's in our magazines, text-books, historical records, official forms, entertainment, classical literature, and beyond. If someone produced it, it's biased; maybe not for the worse but at least by perspective. By simply being exposed to the persistent expression of bias, it's only a matter of time before we internalize those biases into our mental framework.

Bias Can Work in Unexpected Ways...

Mean Girls Mythology

As a former teacher in Baltimore City, I handled a myriad of rewarding (and challenging) daily job duties. I did not think, in truth, with some of my own implicit biases about White women, e.g., that whole *Mean Girls* (2004) thing, I would be able to work closely alongside them; however, when *some* people from my own ingroup, i.e., African-American teachers, failed to help a brother when I needed it, I sometimes depended on my contrasting colleagues.

In short, Zora Neale Hurston was right when she said, 'All my skinfolk ain't kinfolk,' and everyone deserves a fair chance to change the lives of the children we serve. You just never know who is going to be your best partner and ally in this work!

– Brandon Wallace

Humans also form biases through culture, family, experiences, and even by trying not to be biased (Gibson, Rochat, Tone, & Baron; 2017; Rudman, Phelan, & Heppen, 2007). While in teacher and administrator training programs, we learn that families and culture are central to our students' identities and expectations of education. We also consider what happens after school: are kids hungry, well cared for, disciplined, well off, etc.? Just as we need to consider all of these influencers in our students, we need to consider the same in ourselves. What is your cultural identity? What was your experience with X? This could be difficult to manage at first, but it's an important challenge to consider when exploring the roots of bias. Taking this exploration a step further involves understanding your own history and experiences. What were the demographics of the neighborhood that you grew up in? What kinds of impressions have people made on you throughout your life? Taken together, it is not surprising that biases exist but rather surprising that they don't impact *all* of our thoughts and decisions.

If we were to go through life working only off our biases, all of our clothes would be the same color and fabric. We would drink and eat the same few things. We couldn't even read (the letter A doesn't always sound like "ah"). Making decisions based on biases – both implicit and explicit – is a critical part of our everyday life. But just as we are influenced by biases, we can also work hard not to follow our biases (and create new, more positive biases in doing so). Consider your probable bias for sugary foods: you likely do not give in to this bias and actively work to counter the bias. In fact, you may have created a strong bias for not eating sugary foods – an explicit bias. You head to the kitchen and unconsciously go for the cookies, but your explicit bias makes you redirect to the carrot sticks. You might exclusively snack on healthy foods at this point and will one day do so without thinking – that's when it becomes implicit.

While correcting for biases can be beneficial, we must also be wary of simply trying to ignore or dismiss our biases due to backfire effects (Apfelbaum, Norton, & Sommers, 2012; Kang & Lane, 2010; Richeson & Nussbaum, 2004). For example, if you have ever heard the phrase, "I don't see color," you might be familiar with the idea of "colorblindness" as it pertains to racial identity. While you don't want to act on your biases, color-blinding does not allow for consideration of students' individuality and uniqueness. This is just one example of how an effort to counter bias can cause harm by not addressing issues of race directly. While this makes accounting for biases seem very tricky, there are effective ways of remediating bias that will be discussed in Part III. We focus now on seeing bias so that we can know better what we try to avoid.

What Does a Bias Look Like?

While identifying bias in action becomes both a challenging and loaded task, researchers have developed ways to effectively measure both implicit and explicit biases. Due to the nature of bias, tests must be designed to evaluate a particular bias such as racial or body-type bias. In this chapter, we will focus on racial bias although many of these measures have alternative versions to consider other biases ranging from body image to flowers-versus-insects. Understandably, many individuals want to avoid admitting to an explicitly held racial bias, even when told their responses are confidential (Schuman, Steeh, Bobo, & Krysan, 1997). This is why measures such as the Modern Racism Scale or the Symbolic Racism Scale were developed – to unearth covert (i.e., hidden) explicit bias (Henry & Sears, 2002; McConahay, 1986). For example, one agree/disagree item on the Symbolic Racism 2000 Scale reads: "Irish, Italian, Jewish and many other minorities overcame prejudice and worked their way up. Blacks should do the same" (Henry & Sears, 2002, Item #2). Although this question doesn't directly assess positive or negative attitudes toward Black individuals, it does offer a more indirect way to assess biased attitudes toward racial groups. However, these tools are still fundamentally different from those that assess implicit biases – which measure preferences that reside outside of our conscious awareness or control.

Three major measures are used in modern educational research to quantify implicit bias: the Implicit Association Test (Greenwald, McGhee, & Schwartz, 1998), the Affective Priming Task (Fazio, Sanbonmatsu, Powell, & Kardes, 1986), and the Affect Misattribution Procedure (Payne, Cheng, Govorun, & Stewart, 2005), with the Implicit Association Test being most widely used. While each is used to evaluate implicit bias, none of the measures actually measures bias, *per se* – instead, the tools measure preferences, or positive/negative associations in some form. Researchers take these associations to indicate pro-White or pro-African American biases because positive associations are typical of preferences and vice versa. Like the sugar example earlier, if sweets are thought of positively we go to them without thinking. When we associate sweets with bad, we typically go for the carrots. The implicit nature of these findings is where the format of each test becomes more important.

Implicit Association Test

In the Implicit Association Test, a user is shown various stimuli and instructed to categorize each based on categories on the right or left-hand side of a computer monitor. The first set of stimuli are typically positive and negative words. Next, a set of images representing two distinct categories are shown such as insects and flowers; these are again sorted. After some practice, combinations are presented where the user must match the categories (flower vs. bug) with either positive or negative sets of words. The participant's bias is measured by looking at response times for how quickly they form these associations. For example, if participants are more quick to match flowers (vs. bugs) with positive words such as "pleasant" or "good" and slower to match flowers with negative words, the test would reveal a pro-flower bias. Figure 2.2 offers a visualization of the process in more detail with pixelated versions of the images from the juvenile race Implicit Association Test, which features Black and White faces instead of flowers and insects. The test is scored by comparing the correct-response reaction times on the two sets of combination trials. On the race Implicit Association Test, a score close to +1 indicates a strong association between White faces and positive words while a score approaching -1 indicates a strong association between African American faces and positive words (Greenwald, McGhee, & Schwartz, 1998; Greenwald, Nosek, & Banaji, 2003). As you might deduce, a near-zero score reflects no associations (typically noted as no preference). Providing that the test-taker prefers positive words (as nearly all humans do), it is safe to say that one prefers the noted race.

Some criticize that the initially shown combination will always be the preferred combination; however, even when African Americans with positive words are always introduced first, responses tend to show a pro-White preference (Xu, Nosek, & Greenwald, 2013). No measure of bias is perfect, and – like any assessment – the Implicit Association Test has its fair share of

Figure 2.2 The Implicit Association Test consists of five different tasks: (1) word sort, (2) image sort, (3) combined image and word sort, (4) reversed image sort, (5) reversed combined image and word sort

pros and cons. However, due to its popularity as a free and publicly available format, the Implicit Association Test is by far the most widely used tool, which also means that there have been more opportunities to validate its consistency and accuracy.

Affective Priming Task

The Affective Priming Task is based on the widely accepted priming paradigm in psychology which states that people respond more quickly to stimuli when they are preceded by a similar stimulus. Affective priming applies this to positive and negative affects, or feelings, such that people respond more quickly to a positive stimulus when it is presented following another positive stimulus (and vice versa). For example, affective priming would posit quicker responses to the word "happiness" if presented with a smiling baby just prior to the word. In these associations, the primed individual does not make a conscious connection between the stimuli, but the emotional congruence facilitates lower reaction times. This emotional response offers a way to measure implicit associations due to the presence of affective priming effects even when priming stimuli are presented so quickly that they cannot be consciously processed (Fazio et al. 1986; Klauer & Musch, 2003). Again, this is not a direct measure of implicit bias, but rather offers a measure of how strongly associated a target stimulus is to either a positive or negative affect.

The presentation of the Affective Priming Task is much more variable due to the test's more versatile applications in psychological research; however, the pattern of presentation is consistent (Naccache & Dehaene, 2001). Participants are instructed to categorize words as unpleasant or pleasant and shown a focus screen ("***" or "X") prior to each word. After all words are sorted, the participants are told they are to repeat the same task but this time will see a picture rather than the focus screen. The participants are instructed to categorize the word only and not the picture, and then they repeat the task as shown in Figure 2.3. Each set of priming pairs (e.g., target A to pleasant and target B to pleasant) are compared to indicate differences in associations such that one target is identified as more or less strongly associated with the pleasant affect and vice versa. In other words, pleasant feelings are matched to one of the targets more than that other target.

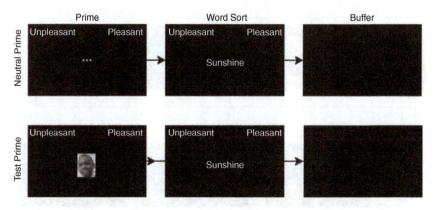

Figure 2.3 In the Affective Priming Task, participants complete the same word task
primed with a neutral item in the first phase and a test item (e.g., African
American and White American faces) in the second phase

Affect Misattribution Procedure

The Affect Misattribution Procedure is the newest of the implicit
measurements discussed in this book and is based on yet another paradigm
of implicit processing, affect misattribution. Affect misattribution posits that
individuals wrongly attribute feelings to one stimulus that were driven by
a prior stimulus (Payne, Hall, Cameron, & Bishara, 2010). You may have
experienced this in your daily life: you wake up and watch the news, make
a cup of coffee, and head out. You find yourself in a grumpy mood and
think that maybe you made decaf coffee by accident, but really you only
heard bad news on this morning's show without even realizing it. This is
affect misattribution – an implicit process tied to our daily lives.

The Affect Misattribution Procedure plays off the very large effect
of this implicit process by using potentially positive or negative stimuli
(African American or White, skinny or fat, flowers or insects, etc.) just prior
to presenting neutral stimuli, typically Chinese characters for those who
cannot read Chinese (Payne, & Lundberg, 2014; Payne et al., 2005). This
test is different than the other tests in that there is no reading or cognitive processing involved during the presentation of the images, but rather
afterwards. As demonstrated in Figure 2.4, the user is focused on a screen
like in the Affective Priming Task, which quickly flashes the target stimulus
(sometimes for a subconscious duration), a blank screen, the neutral

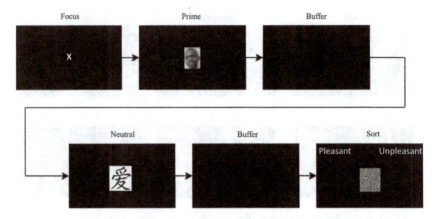

Figure 2.4 All images in the Affect Misattribution Procedure are presented in less than one second. The participant is instructed to sort only the Chinese character and even warned about the potential bias from the primed image

stimulus, another blank screen, and then a noise image (think static). After those are all presented (in less than one second), the user rates the neutral stimulus as positive or negative. The test is scored by looking at how often each target was followed by positive or negative ratings of the neutral stimuli and looking for differences. Here, the response made (rather than the response latency) is used to calculate the score, unlike the previously discussed measures (Payne & Lundberg, 2014; Payne et al., 2005). The Affect Misattribution Procedure continues to grow in popularity and use as a quicker assessment than the Implicit Association Test or Affective Priming Task.

What's the Best Way to Look at *My* Bias?

With the expansion of implicit bias research into more and more fields of study, the Implicit Association Test continues to experience the widest usage (Nosek, Hawkins, & Frazier, 2011), possibly due to its free accessibility through Harvard's Project Implicit (see Project Implicit, 2011) or the extensive reliability and validity data available through both psychometric and prior usage study. The Implicit Association Test (and Sequential Priming Task) reflect four separate elements of implicit bias: association activation, bias moderation, controlled processing, and guessing (Conrey, Sherman,

Gawronski, Hugenberg, & Groom, 2005). These contributive components may provide a better understanding of how implicit bias acts in realistic situations, but may also cloud evaluations specific to just implicit bias. Furthermore, tests like the Implicit Association Test and the Affective Priming Task can take more time to complete than shorter tasks such as the Affect Misattribution Procedure. In sum, choosing a measure of implicit bias depends greatly on how and what you are interested in measuring and eventually doing with that information.

Summary

Implicit bias is not a simple phenomenon. The forces, sources, and discourses involved embody intricate processes that often feel lofty and overly complicated; however, implicit bias is an understandable and natural part of our daily lives. With neurological roots embedded in categorization, implicit bias acts as a natural efficiency mechanism in many situations. Unfortunately, various forces work to develop these implicit categorization into damaging biases that create inequities and social challenges. As such, methods to inform the discourse of implicit bias have been developed. These measures offer insight into how our unconscious categorizations create positive and negative situations that influence the world around us. With an understanding of implicit bias, we can move forward to better comprehend the impacts of such bias on our students.

References

Allen, S. F. (2015, November 24). Media bias: 8 types [Think Tank]. Retrieved from https://capitalresearch.org/article/media-bias-8-types-a-classic-kinda/

Amodio, D. (2014). The neuroscience of prejudice and stereotyping. *Nature Reviews Neuroscience, 15*, 670–682. https://doi.org/10.1038/nrn3800

Apfelbaum, E. P., Norton, M. I., & Sommers, S. R. (2012). Racial color blindness: Emergence, practice, and implications. *Current Directions in Psychological Science, 21*(3), 205–209.

Baker, B. (1994). *How to identify, expose, & correct liberal media bias.* Alexandria, VA: Media Research Center.

Botvinick, M. M., Cohen, J. D., & Carter, C. (2004). Conflict monitoring and anterior cingulate cortex: An update. *Trends in Cognitive Sciences, 8*(12), 539–546.

Conrey, F. R., Sherman, J. W., Gawronski, B., Hugenberg, K., & Groom, C. J. (2005). Separating multiple processes in implicit social cognition: The quad model of implicit task performance. *Journal of Personality and Social Psychology, 89*(4), 469–487.

Cristofori, I., Zhong, W., Mandoske, V., Chau, A., Krueger, F., Strenziok, M., & Grafman, J. (2016). Brain regions influencing implicit violent attitudes: A lesion-mapping study. *The Journal of Neuroscience, 36*(9), 2757–2768. https://doi.org/10.1523/JNEUROSCI.2975-15.2016

Derks, B., Stedehouder, J., & Ito, T. A. (2015). Social identity modifies face perception: An ERP study of social categorization. *Social Cognitive and Affective Neuroscience, 10*(5), 672–679. https://doi.org/10.1093/scan/nsu107

Farah, M. J. (2000). The neural bases of mental imagery. In M. S. Gazzaniga (Ed), The cognitive neurosciences (2nd ed.) (pp. 965–974). Cambridge, MA: MIT Press.

Fazio, R. H., Sanbonmatsu, D. M., Powell, M. C., & Kardes, F. R. (1986). On the automatic activation of attitudes. *Journal of Personality and Social Psychology, 50*(2), 229–238.

Gibson, B. L., Rochat, P., Tone, E. B., & Baron, A. S. (2017). Sources of implicit and explicit intergroup race bias among African-American children and young adults. *PLOS ONE, 12*(9), e0183015. https://doi.org/10.1371/journal.pone.0183015

Greenwald, A. G., McGhee, D. E., & Schwartz, J. L. (1998). Measuring individual differences in implicit cognition: The implicit association test. *Journal of Personality and Social Psychology, 74*(6), 1464–1480.

Greenwald, A. G., Nosek, B. A., & Banaji, M. R. (2003). Understanding and using the Implicit Association Test: I. An improved scoring algorithm. *Journal of Personality and Social Psychology, 85*(2), 197–216.

Healy, G. F., Boran, L., & Smeaton, A. F. (2015). Neural patterns of the Implicit Association Test. *Frontiers in Human Neuroscience, 9*, 605. https://doi.org/10.3389/fnhum.2015.00605

Hehman, E., Volpert, H. I., & Simons, R. F. (2014). The N400 as an index of racial stereotype accessibility. *Social Cognitive and Affective Neuroscience, 9*(4), 544–552. https://doi.org/10.1093/scan/nst018

Henry, P. J., & Sears, D. O. (2002). They symbolic racism 2000 scale. *Political Psychology*, *23*(2), 253–283.

Hinton, P. (2017). Implicit stereotypes and the predictive brain: Cognition and culture in "biased" person perception. *Palgrave Communications*, *3*, 17086.

Hugenberg, K., & Bodenhausen, G. (2003). Facing prejudice: Implicit prejudice and the perception of facial threat. *Psychological Science*, *14*(6), 640–643.

Kang, J., & Lane, K. (2010). Seeing through colorblindness: Implicit bias and the law. *UCLA Law Review*, *58*, 465–520.

Klauer, K. C., & Musch, J. (2003). Affective priming: Findings and theories. In J. Musch & K .C. Klauer (Eds.), *The psychology of evaluation: Affective processes in cognition and emotion* (pp. 7–49). Mahwah, NJ: Erlbaum.

McConahay, J. B. (1986). Modern racism, ambivalence, and the Modern Racism Scale. In J. F. Dovidio & S. L. Gaertner (Eds.), *Prejudice, discrimination, and racism* (pp. 91–125). San Diego, CA: Academic Press.

Mitchell, J. P., Ames, D. L., Jenkins, A. C., & Banaji, M. R. (2009). Neural correlates of stereotype application. *Journal of Cognitive Neuroscience*, *21*, 594–604.

Molenberghs, P., & Morrison, S. (2014). The role of the medial prefrontal cortex in social categorization. *Social Cognitive and Affective Neuroscience*, *9*(3), 292–296.

Naccache, L., & Dehaene, S. (2001). Unconscious semantic priming extends to novel unseen stimuli. *Cognition*, *80*, 215–229.

Neal, L. I., McCray, A. D., Webb-Johnson, G., & Bridgest, S. T. (2003). The effects of African American movement styles on teachers' perceptions and reactions. *The Journal of Special Education*, *37*(1), 49–57.

Nosek, B. A., Hawkins, C. B., & Frazier, R. S. (2011). Implicit social cognition: From measures to mechanisms. *Trends in Cognitive Sciences*, *15*(4), 152–159.

Payne, B. K., Cheng, C. M., Govorun, O., & Stewart, B. D. (2005). An inkblot for attitudes: Affect misattribution as implicit measurement. *Journal of Personality and Social Psychology*, *89*(3), 277–293.

Payne, B. K., Hall, D. L., Cameron, C. D., & Bishara, A. J. (2010). A process model of affect misattribution. *Personality and Social Psychology Bulletin*, *36*(10), 1397–1408.

Payne, K., & Lundberg, K. (2014). The affect misattribution procedure: Ten years of evidence on reliability, validity, and mechanisms. *Social and Personality Psychology Compass, 8*(12), 672–686.

Pickett, J. A., & Chiricos, T. (2012). Controlling other people's' children: Racialized views of delinquency and Whites' punitive attitudes toward juvenile children. *Criminology, 50*(3), 673–710.

Project Implicit. (2011). Take a Test. Retrieved from https://implicit.harvard.edu/implicit/takeatest.html

Richeson, J. A., & Nussbaum, R. J. (2004). The impact of multiculturalism versus color-blindness on racial bias. *Journal of Experimental Social Psychology, 40*, 417–423.

Rudman, L. A. (2004a). Social justice in our minds, homes, and society: The nature, causes, and consequences of implicit bias. *Social Justice Research, 17*(2), 129–142.

Rudman, L. A. (2004b). Sources of implicit attitudes. *Current Directions in Psychological Science, 13*(2), 79–82. https://doi.org/10.1111/j.0963-7214.2004.00279.x

Rudman, L. A., Phelan, J. E., & Heppen, J. B. (2007). Developmental sources of implicit attitudes. *Personality and Social Psychology Bulletin, 33*(12), 1700–1713.

Schuman, H., Steeh, C., Bobo, L., & Krysan, M. (1997). *Racial attitudes in America: Trends and interpretations*. Cambridge, MA: Harvard University Press.

Stanley, D., Phelps, E., & Banaji, B. (2008). The neural basis of implicit attitudes. *Current Directions in Psychological Science, 17*(2), 164–170. https://doi.org/10.1111/j.1467-8721.2008.00568.x

Stroop, J. R. (1935). Studies of interference in serial verbal reactions. *Journal of Experimental Psychology, 18*, 643–662.

Williams, J. K., & Themanson, J. R. (2011). Neural correlates of the implicit association test: Evidence for semantic and emotional processing. *Social Cognitive and Affective Neuroscience, 6*(4), 468–476. https://doi.org/10.1093/scan/nsq065

Xu, K., Nosek, B. A., & Greenwald, A. G. (2013). *Race IAT 2002–2013* [dataset]. Retrieved from https://osf.io/52qxl/

Why Does Implicit Bias Matter?

3

Making the Grade
Academics

Introduction

> We all have *that one student* in our class who makes the day seem longer.
> – Heard in the teacher's lounge while substitute teaching

Call "that one student" what you will: challenge, EBD, troublemaker, the one who needs more time; but the moment he or she has a label, chances are bias will follow. Sometimes the best intentions don't lead to the best outcomes. As educators we want our students to do well. We don't get into teaching to keep the some students down or make sure our kids do better than the rest – at least not intentionally. Nevertheless, we find our attempts at academically saving our students leading to more and more academic decline. Often such declines are linked with time limitations: we can only spend so much time working with one student before that focus reciprocally takes much-needed attention from other students. However, academic declines sometimes stem from teachers' expectations of their

A **self-fulfilling prophecy** refers to the tendency of individuals to behave in ways that mirror the expectations that they perceived others to hold toward them. For students, self-fulfilling prophecies often mean working more or less diligently to achieve academically based on the student's experience of academic expectations from teachers, parents, and other authoritative figures.

students. We contribute to our students' **self-fulfilling prophecies** of mediocrity when we come in with expectations that their academic potential is somehow "less than." Consider the phrases in Table 3.1: each educator wants to help students, but the complement to each sentence is alarming.

While these implied statements are extreme, they reflect the version of the statements often felt by those *other students* in schools. We all hold implicit perceptions of who is the "other" or outside of our ingroup. Our perceptions vary, but often we consider the outsider kids to be those labeled with special needs who really need extra support, the non-Asian students in the math classroom, the boys in English Language Arts, the girls in science, the heavier students in Physical Education. In every classroom, perceptions of who is considered "at risk" affect students from low socioeconomic status (SES) families, immigrant communities, and students with darker skin. For example, educators never sit down and say, "Hakima is a recently immigrated African American girl, so she can't possibly get above a D+ in Biology." However, the same educators might see the new student on the roster and suggest she start off in the low-level science track, "in case she needs extra time." In better situations, the school might send

Table 3.1 Teacher Statements and Implications

What the Teacher Says…	*What the Statement Implies…*
"I try to give them problems that they can solve to build their confidence."	"If I give them the standard problems, the students will fail. I want them to think that they can do well."
"They don't really get read to at home. How can I expect them to keep up with the others?"	"These kids' parents can't read to them, and that makes the kids incapable of catching up."
"I know they work hard, and that's enough for me."	"It's not important to me if students do well as long as they put out a lot of effort."
"Maybe if I offer them extra credit for coming to the event, they can bring up their grades."	"They can't achieve high grades through mastery of the material, so I need to let them fake it in other ways."
"If my class is half *those* students, then it hurts the other half of the students who *can* do it."	"If my class is half *those* students, they will keep all my good students from doing well."
"We track the kids to let the good ones do better and give the kids something at their own level."	"We track the kids to let the poor ones do worse. We can only give them material that kids 'like that' can complete."

Hakima for science testing, maybe even in her primary language; however, very few schools will simply put her on the standard science track. This is implicit bias in action and shows us just one of the potential routes to academic impact.

Of course, not all implicit bias-linked academic effects stem from teacher expectations. Bias also exists in the materials we use through a lacking presence of cultural relevance in the curriculum (see Table 3.2 for forms of curriculum bias). Bias can come into play through a cultural/racial mismatch between teachers and students such as a misunderstanding of religious practices as excuses to leave the classroom. Bias presents through the geo-political school zoning lines and related gerrymandering (redistricting election zones to favor one political party) that often segregates schools by race and/or SES. Bias comes through higher pedagogical expertise of high SES district teachers and teacher performance under stressful conditions such as large class sizes and political unrest. Bias even has a way of making itself into mentoring, college acceptance, writing style judgements, and student employment as we will discuss later in this chapter. If human judgement is involved, bias is involved; when bias is involved in judgements related to achievement, we have the potential to influence the success of our students.

Going forward we will begin by exploring various definitions of student achievement before looking at the impacts of implicit bias on achievement at a classroom- and school-wide level. We will briefly touch on community-wide impacts to achievement, but as the focus of this book is on schools an extensive discussion is not possible. We end with the academic to discipline link before moving into Chapter 4, which focuses on the impacts of implicit bias on discipline.

Measuring Achievement

When we think of how to define student achievement, most want students to exert effort, demonstrate skills, and have courage (or grit) that results in success; however, this brings us only to the act of defining success. While an exploration of the various definitions of student success from state and national assessments, long-term outcomes, and so forth is outside the scope of this book, most simply want to provide students with tools and strategies to do... perhaps anything. While we cannot take such a broad definition of achievement in research, we *can* consider the implications of research to this broader definition of success with a focus on bettering our understanding and quality of service toward ALL students.

How do researchers define achievement? This large concept is often debated; however, three basic methods are most often employed in educational and sociological research: standardized test scores, student grades/criterion-test scores, and access. Both score-related measures tend to assess math and reading distinctly and infrequently evaluate achievement as it relates to other school domains of learning such as science, technology, social studies, or writing. Grades and criterion-test scores are typically more variable than standardized test scores (i.e., state assessments, SATs) due to inherent teacher subjectivity (think open-ended questions) and the presence of non-value-added contributors such as extra credit for event attendance. Access relates to a broad classification of achievement measures inclusive of specialized program enrollment, job attainment, college acceptance, on-time high school graduation, and some elements of quality of life. As illustrated in Figure 3.1, together these measures make up a multifaceted concept of student achievement in the educational research literature as it relates to potential implicit bias.

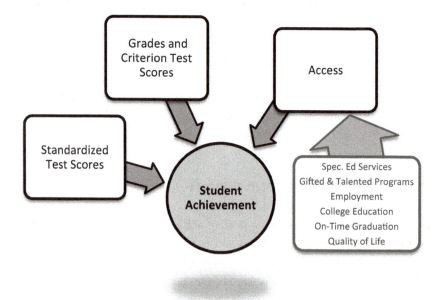

Figure 3.1 The visual representation of student achievement above shows the three methods of student achievement assessment most often seen in the research literature

Classroom-Level Implicit Bias

Teacher Expectations

By far the most widely researched mechanism for classroom-level implicit bias is teacher expectations of students and differences in these expectations by both race/ethnicity and gender. As early as 1970, educational research began to explore the impacts of teacher expectations on student outcomes through differences in teacher behavior (Rist, 2000). In this first study, teachers differed distinctively in their expectations of slow and quick learners, which manifested in differences in how often they used positive reinforcement with their students. Using positive reinforcement more or less depending on whether the teacher saw students as slow or quick learners led students to behave more in ways that reflected the teachers' expectations and soon led to teachers being reinforced in the validity of the expectations. See Figure 3.2 for a visual application of the patterns found in the Rist (2000) study.

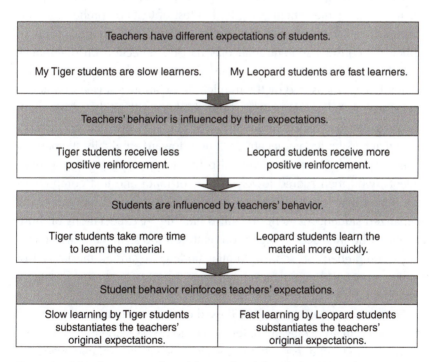

Figure 3.2 Visual representation of the results of the Rist (2000) study

As time went on, studies focused more on expectation differences by race and gender, finding that teacher expectations were lower for students of minority races overall and lowest for minority male students – especially those who were "non-submissive" and "independent" (Ross & Jackson, 1991). Later researchers found that teacher expectation differences by race were often reflective of actual differences (Jussim & Eccles, 1992; Jussim, Eccles, & Madon, 1996); however, as time went on these findings dissipated and racial expectation differences were no longer accounted for by actual (biological) differences but stemmed from social factors instead (Ferguson, 2003; Friedrich, Flunger, Nagengast, Jonkmann, & Trautwein, 2015; Tenenbaum & Ruck, 2007). Whether this shift is reflective of better measurement tools, differences in student ability possibly related to other biasing factors, the growing cacophony of potential ability factors, or another mechanism remains unclear; however, teacher expectation bias seems to match teachers' levels of implicit bias and explain a significant amount of the differences in academic achievement by race/ethnicity (Van den Bergh, Denessen, Hornstra, Voeten, & Holland, 2010).

Van den Bergh's 2010 study of teacher expectations and implicit bias measured achievement using both a test of text comprehension and a standardized math assessment. While teachers' self-reported levels of explicit (or conscious/intentional) bias had no reflection on differences in student achievement by race on either measure of achievement, implicit bias as measured by the Implicit Association Test (see Chapter 2) helped to predict differences in both reading and math achievement by way of teacher expectations (full mediation for the statistics lovers). When teachers had more negative attitudes toward ethnically stigmatized students (Turkish/Moroccan), they also had lower expectations of those students, who then scored lower on tests of math and text comprehension. When teachers had more positive attitudes toward non-ethnically stigmatized students (Dutch), they also had higher expectations of those students, who then scored higher on math test (no significant differences in text comprehension scores). Similar findings regarding the impact of teacher expectations on achievement were found in longitudinal data by Friedrich and his team (2015).

Friedrich and colleagues (2015) used end-of-year grades in math and standardized math achievement test scores to assess student achievement as it related to teacher expectations. Their research showed that even after considering differences in student age, gender, and prior achievement (based on prior grades, a figurative reasoning task, and a baseline standardized math test), teachers' expectations of students predicted differences in achievement. Practically stated, teachers' expectations explained differences in achievement even after ruling out the developmental and academic differences between the students – teacher expectations seemed to affect student achievement. Interestingly, these findings were found when looking at students individually and not when comparing classes based on the teacher's average expectations for the class. Furthermore, the students' self-concept, or personal expectations and self-esteem, explained some of this relationship (partially mediated), bringing to light why many studies might find that teacher expectations affect stigmatized-group students more strongly.

Ferguson (2003) suggested that the greater impact of teacher expectations on students of stigmatized groups, typically students of Color in the U.S., could result from an interaction with students' beliefs, behaviors, and work habits. He extrapolated that stereotype threat (fear of becoming the stereotype one is perceived as embodying) could increase student anxiety to perpetuate the achievement gap between Black and White students. In support of Ferguson's model, Woolley and colleagues (2010) found that as teacher expectations increased, student anxiety decreased and that lower anxiety resulted in higher SAT scores and math grades. They further found that higher teacher expectations were consistent with higher levels of student confidence and subject interest, where high confidence was linked with more hours studying for math, higher SAT scores, and higher math grades (subject interest only with higher grades). Considered together, these studies provide a clear mechanism for the teacher expectations to student achievement link, especially as it related to racial differences, as seen in Figure 3.3.

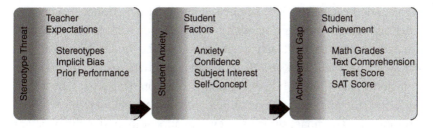

Figure 3.3 Teacher expectation pathway with potential influencers (based on Wooley [2010]) as it relates to Ferguson's (2003) stereotype threat model

Implicitly Biased Reactions

'Hey… Stop! You can't go there.'

I hear the security guard yelling as I pass on the way to the bathroom. I hear him yelling, but since I'm just walking to the women's room, I ignore him. I have to use the facilities and can't imagine he is yelling at me – why couldn't I go in the bathroom? I enter and find an open stall.

Bang, bang, bang. He starts banging on the door.

Bang, bang, bang. 'That's the women's room. Get out of there.'

I open the door to face him. 'I know, I *am* a woman.' I wish I could slam the door, but it's not the slamming type, so I turn around and go back into the stall.

Reflecting afterwards, I was stunned. I go through this lobby daily, and though I have very short hair and often wear a hood, my facial features and body type are almost always read as cis-gender female, which I am. What do students who are transgender or non-gender conforming experience when they go to the bathroom? Who is actually unsafe; who is actually threatened?

– Rachel Roegman

In accepting that teacher expectations transfer to student achievement, the consideration of how much teacher expectations reflect biases remains subject to debate. In addition to Van den Bergh's (2010) findings relating teachers' implicit bias to differences by ethnicity in teachers' expectations of students, Gershenson, Holt, and Papageorge (2016) found a link between racial mismatch and student expectations. Non-Black teachers of Black students held lower expectations of Black students than Black teachers of Black students – especially for male students and by math teachers. This might underlie Dee's (2004) findings that students perform significantly better on math and reading standardized tests when a student and teacher are of the same race, but teacher expectations go beyond just racial match. McKown and Weinstein (2008) found that teachers' expectations again predicted achievement, but expectations only predicted gaps by ethnicity when students' perceptions of differential treatment were high. While expectations can impact students, they also appear to modify the behavior of the teachers, potentially leading to less effective and more biased instruction.

Teacher Traits

We know that teachers have implicit biases favoring native and lighter-skinned students from several studies and anecdotal accounts (Boysen & Vogel, 2009; Glock & Klapproth, 2017; Glock, Kneer, & Kovacs, 2013; Kumar, Karabenick, & Burgoon, 2015; Peterson, Rubie-Davies, Osborne, & Sibley, 2016). We know that bias changes behavior as a built-in neural process (see Chapter 2). Put these together and you will expect bias to change teacher behavior, and this is exactly what the research tells us.

Take a look at Figure 3.4 as you read on: A group of White teachers are asked to give a short lesson to a either a Black or White learner, and

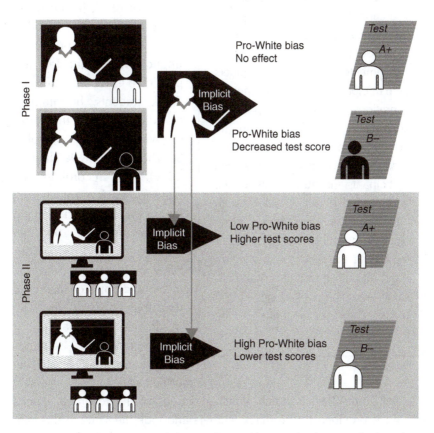

Figure 3.4 Visual depiction of the Jacoby-Senghor study showing that teachers' high pro-White biases created teaching differences that led to lower test scores for Black students

Are Some Studies Better?

While most published research is of high quality, some research designs are more valid than others. When researchers design a quantitative study, they try to use an experimental design that controls for other explanations of the phenomenon they are studying. In human-subjects research this is often difficult because you cannot really control people or even know enough about people to account for all the differences. Experimenters use large numbers of participants and create specific conditions to focus on potential contributors to the phenomenon. The Jacoby-Senghor study described here used many participants, matched participants and students by gender, and created different racial match conditions. They even considered the effect of the students on the teacher by adding the recorded portion of the study. These elements make this study especially well designed and reduce the questionability of the results substantially.

the lesson is audio-visually recorded. After the lesson, teachers complete a measure of their pro-Black or pro-White levels of implicit bias while the students complete a test of the material they just learned in the lesson. Statistics are calculated and it turns out that the teachers' pro-White implicit bias scores predict the diminished test scores of Black learners, but not White learners. In other words, higher pro-White implicit bias of the teachers predicted lower test scores for Black students, but implicit bias did not predict the scores of White students (Jacoby-Senghor, Sinclair, & Shelton, 2016). The recordings are rated for teacher anxiety and lesson quality, which explain the relationship between implicit bias and test scores. We want to jump and say that the implicit bias changed the teaching behavior resulting in lower performance for non-preferred students, but we need (at least) one more check.

Next, non-Black students watched videos of the recorded lessons that were provided to the Black learners and took the same test. Again, implicit bias predicted diminished test performance, and this time it was for non-Black learners. Black learners were *not* simply performing worse than White learners, but instead the lesson provided to these learners was different in some way. While this may sounds like a hypothetical, this study actually occurred with 51 Black learner-White teacher pairs and 54 White learner-White teacher pairs (all gender matched, male-male or female-female) for the lessons, and another 165 students (98% White, 2% non-Black) watching the videos. If you are not a research person, this is a text-book, well-designed study with an ideal number of participants for the kind of statistics and methods used – and it really showed that something was going on.

Other studies linked behavioral changes back to differences in teacher expectations. In 1979, Taylor found that teachers-in-training provided longer response times, lengthier praise, and were less nervous when teaching a student behind a screen that was described as Black than when the student was described as White. A 2008 study by McKown and Weinstein found that even elementary students experienced these effects: differences in teachers' expectations of European American and Asian American students were predicted by whether students perceived a high or low level of differential treatment by teachers toward the high- and low-achievers in the class. When students viewed teachers as treating high- and low-achievers more differently, the teachers' expectations of students based on ethnicities were more stratified. When perceptions of differential treatment were low, these differences by ethnicity in teacher expectations dissipated. Furthermore, a sizable European- to Asian American achievement gap existed only in classrooms with noted differences in perceived (and actual) expectations. Simply showing a preference toward the "smart kids" seemed to lead to academic differences by ethnicity.

School/Community-Level Implicit Bias

Bias in Curricular Materials

Students are faced with bias even before face-to-face interaction occurs through curricular materials such as classroom posters, test items, and text-books. Classroom posters often display gendered stereotypes in student behaviors and dress although the racial and ethnic diversity of such posters continues to increase. Sometimes, posters display information on colleges or on supports available to students in formats that are mostly unbiased,

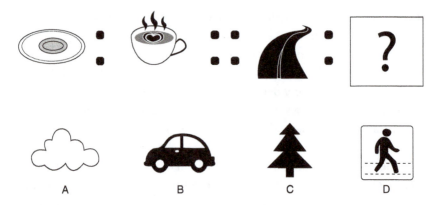

Figure 3.5 Cultural irrelevance in an analogy test item

but the posters are placed in implicitly biased areas such as college posters placed only in AP classrooms and abuse-support posters placed only in multicultural lounges. Test items may become biased through creator biases or a lack of cultural relevancy. Consider the kindergarten analogy test item in Figure 3.5; what answer would you pick?

If you saw the first item as a saucer, like intended, you should choose B: saucers go under teacups and roads go under cars. If you never had any experience with a saucer, like many lower SES students, you might think the item is a plate and choose C or D: plates go next to cups and trees/sidewalks go next to roads. Here no implicit bias is intended, but the test makes implicit assumptions about student knowledge without cultural considerations.

A more expansive area of bias (both implicit and explicit) exists in text-books where potential biases are delineated with seven domains: (1) invisibility, (2) stereotyping, (3) singular interpretation, (4) selective reporting (the rose-colored glasses effect), (5) fragmentation, (6) linguistic bias, and (7) cosmetic bias. Many of these forms of bias mirror those in media bias discussed in the previous chapter in that they relate to who or what is excluded and included in reporting. Others focus more on how information is presented. Table 3.2 provides definitions and examples of each form of text-book bias to help portray how text-books may perpetuate and contribute to implicit bias and the effects of such biases in schools. As we saw in the test item bias, text-book biases often result from cultural misunderstandings and misrepresentations that may be assisted through the inclusion of **culturally responsive practices**.

Table 3.2 Forms of Text-Book Bias

Bias Form	Explanation	Example
Invisibility	Bias by omission; groups of individuals are left out of curricular materials preventing knowledge acquisition.	Many history texts fail to include accounts of Stonewall and the murder of Matthew Shepard in Laramie, WY in avoidance of homosexuality.
Stereotyping	Characterizing individuals from a subgroup based on assumed group traits.	Literature texts that only include stories where women are portrayed as caregivers.
Singular Interpretation	Presenting material with only one perspective of a given phenomenon.	Science texts typically focus on discoveries made by European males.
Selective Reporting (Rose-Colored Glasses Effect)	Glossing over controversial and/or "heated" topics.	Discussion of legislation to increase the rights of people with special needs rather than the issues that led to the need for such laws.
Fragmentation	Placing information about certain subgroups only in boxed text or as special insert sections.	Boxed text of "African American Mathematicians" in a mathematics text omitting elsewhere similar contributions.
Linguistic Bias	Labeling bias; using word connotation to influence feelings about an event. OR Limiting access to material based on language.	Describing affirmative action as providing an *advantage* to people of Color rather than as an *equalizing* practice. OR Use of American idioms in text, creating a greater challenge for English learners.
Cosmetic Bias	Using covers and other eye-catching features to suggest equity.	A literature book featuring several male and female children of various ethnicities on the cover, but including mainly White male authors.

Culturally Responsive Practices

Schools often fail to meet the needs of different ethnic groups through teaching/pedagogy, curriculum, leadership, or overall practices. Geneva Gay offers an in-depth discussion in her 2010 book, *Culturally Responsive Teaching*, which is driven by the following five premises:

1. Culture is central to education.
2. Conventional reforms for increasing the achievement of students of Color are inadequate.
3. Intention without action is insufficient.
4. Cultural diversity is a strength of schools and organizations.
5. Test scores and grades are symptoms of achievement problems and do not explain WHY achievement problems exist.

Many times the defaults in schools directly counter these premises as they relate to meeting the needs of a culturally diverse student body. While school culture refers to an abstract feeling of community and belongingness for many, the essential elements of that culture are often implicitly biased through their historically White developments. Schools have come a long way from the initial days of desegregation, but many schools have used only conventional methods of reform to redefine the school culture toward a more inclusive disposition. Often schools have statements of equity and inclusion with no accountability or action, with some schools continuing to exhibit counter-inclusive behaviors through use of biased curricula that do not develop respect and foster interethnic dialogue. Some say that our students of Color perform poorly on tests because they are "low-achievers," but cultural responsivity asks why and what is causing those students to achieve less.

As a school leader, culturally responsive practices not only focus on what is and is not being done to respect and attend to students' cultures, but also how the school and leadership create an internal culture where these practices are held central. **Culturally Responsive School Leadership** is achieved through four behaviors (Khalifa, Gooden, & Davis, 2016): (1) "critical self-awareness" (p. 1280), (2) "culturally responsive curricula and teacher preparation" (p. 1281), (3) "culturally responsive and inclusive school environments" (p. 1282), and (4) "engaging students and parents in community contexts" (p. 1282). Critically self-aware leaders, "use their understanding [of self and context] to envision and create a new environment of learning for children," and are "aware of inequitable factors that adversely affect their students' potential" (p. 1280). They also can face personal cultural (and racial) assumptions and how those assumptions impact the school. These leaders follow through with responsive curricula and provide professional development and modeling that support teachers' practices. In all of this, such leaders engage students as well as community members and families in order to develop a school-community context that values cultural fluency. Culture is all around us but in our haste to education, we often unconsciously and unintentionally forget to respond to *ALL* cultures – sometimes starting with our own.

Culturally Responsive Teaching is how **Culturally Responsive Practices** can be achieved in classroom relations, but culturally responsive practices also go beyond the student–teacher relationship. When assessing the school for cultural responsiveness consider the following questions:

1. Are there opportunities for families, and community members to become involved in class activities?
2. How often do teachers and administrators make positive contact with student families?
3. What might limit families from participating in school-related activities both during and outside of school hours? How do you provide opportunities that overcome these challenges?
4. Does the school make multiple attempts in different forms (phone call, email, home language) to involve families in events and decisions?
5. How does the school use community resources to encourage and support families that are hesitant to become involved in school functions?
6. What does the school do to get to know the community? What should teachers and administrators do to learn more and contribute?
7. How does the school approach students with native languages other than English? Does this treat the language as an asset?

8. Does the school celebrate special events in students' lives? How does the school determine what events are special to different students?

9. What supports are in place to encourage collaboration between teachers, special education teachers, and support staff? How are community organizations involved in these collaborations?

10. Does the school's curricula include culturally responsive materials and content that is relevant to the school's student populations?

11. What information sources are used to make instructional and behavior support decisions? What other elements need to be considered in these decisions? What stakeholders are currently left out?

12. Are different kinds of instruction used that allow different kinds of learners to access the material in ways that meet their individual needs?

13. How do the school, teachers, and administrators motivate students to become active learners and critical reflectors? What is done to facilitate social and political understanding?

14. Does the school acknowledge both the similarities *and the differences* between students and families in ways that build cultural competence and mutual respect?

15. How does the school approach social skills and problem-solving skills instruction? Do all students get access?

16. What is included in teacher–family conference discussions? How do teachers and families learn about expectations, customs, and behavior management practices at home and at school? Are differences considered when planning instruction and policy?

17. How does the school make sure that all students (by race, culture, gender, ethnicity, home language, ability, etc.) are recognized for their work accomplishments? Are all students given the same encouragement and opportunities to become involved in school and extracurricular activities?

18. What does the school do to avoid treating individuals as representatives for their entire subgroup?

19. How do students and families safely report and respond to perceived and/or experienced inequities?
20. How does the school maintain communication with families (and students, as appropriate) over the summer?

(Based on Griner & Stewart, 2013)

These questions can be edited to meet the specific needs and challenges that face your school and act as a starting point when understanding what culturally responsive practices mean for your individual school.

Accessibility

Growing up as a Black male, I had very limited exposure to White people during my childhood. That changed drastically my kindergarten year when I went to a predominantly White school. This experience shaped my perception of what school was; I knew that I was one of the few Black students, but I didn't feel out of place.

When I eventually switched schools, my perception of what school was shifted too. The school I transitioned to was completely different: the environment, the quality of books, the food, the energy. Most of all, I noticed the race of children was different as I went from a predominantly White to predominantly Black school.

In both of these settings, most of my teachers were White females. At my last school, I had had mostly positive interactions and views of these teachers. This is why I came into the new school with a belief that teachers, like other authority figures, should be respected and listened to. But, I began to feel singled out by White women because I was continuously punished for things that I didn't do – I was considered guilty by association with my peers. So I began to punish myself by putting myself in timeout during recess and not speaking during class. Eventually, I developed a bias toward White women because I figured they disliked Black children.

– Donte Wood-Spikes

Students often attend schools where most of the students look like they do. Table 3.3 shows the percentage of same-race students and

Table 3.3 Percentage of Same-Race and Free-Lunch Students by Student Ethnicity and School Type

Ethnicity	Elementary		High School	
	Same-Race	Free-Lunch	Same-Race	Free-Lunch
White	61.0	42.9	59.1	35.8
Black	56.1	74.7	50.7	67.1
Hispanic	61.9	69.1	57.9	56.4

Note: Numbers indicate the percentage of students of the same race or percentage of students eligible for free lunch (across ethnicities) characteristic of schools attended by noted ethnicity students.

free-or-reduced-lunch eligible students by ethnicity and school level who are enrolled in U.S. public, non-charter schools according to 2011–12 National Center for Educational Statistics Data (Logan & Burdick-Will, 2016). While schools are not exclusive, clear patterns of resegregation are apparent in this trend of majority same-race students. With students of Color experiencing much higher poverty levels than White students (as indicated by free-and-reduced-lunch eligibility), tax-dollars connected to these rates perpetuate a school resource imbalance that often results in lower-quality teachers, fewer academic resources, and higher student–teacher ratios in schools serving non-White students. While this fact is not inherently linked to implicit bias, it may result from decades of implicitly (and explicitly) biased decisions, including where individuals have the opportunity to buy houses and send their children to school. There is not much a school leader can do to counteract these neighborhood-level inequities, but other elements of accessibility are under the umbrella of school leaders' sway.

Students of Color are over-represented in special educational programs (Reschley, 1997), under-represented in gifted and talented programs (Goings, & Ford, 2018; Grissom & Redding, 2015), and often cannot receive appropriate accommodations in college (Yull, 2015). Even when only considering high-test-score students, Black students are less likely to be enrolled in gifted and talented programs and even less likely to be referred for gifted and talented by non-Black teachers (Grisson & Redding, 2015). While there is not much research about how these inequities are perpetuated (Goings & Ford, 2018), many of the concepts related to teacher expectations and cultural relevance can be theoretically extrapolated to the consideration of the barrier to gifted and talented program enrollment. If students cannot access programs at unbiased rates, they are unlikely to excel to their maximum potential. Chapter 6 will highlight ways that school leaders can manage data using equity audits to foster more equitable program enrollment.

Although college is beyond the K-12 school environment, school leaders can work to prepare students to challenge discrimination in appropriate ways that are lucrative to college acceptance and success. To start, college admission essays appear implicitly biased as admission essay scoring favors masculine writing styles (Magee, 2015). In a study of college mentor seeking, only male students with traditionally White names received noteworthy response rates to emails sent inquiring about meetings with potential college professor mentors (Milkman, Akinola, & Chugh, 2015). In a study of one medical school, admissions workers admitted to thinking bias may have impacted their acceptance rates (Capers, Clinchot, McDougle, & Greenwald, 2017). After taking and responding to implicit bias measures, the following admissions cycle yielded the most ethnically diverse class the school had ever accepted. Access to college is omnipresent as a barrier to student success and is only confounded by implicit biases, but school leaders are in a position to meet the needs of students experiencing such bias through targeted trainings and mentorship opportunities.

The Academic–Discipline Link

In a pivotal 2010 article, a team of researchers called the achievement and discipline gaps "two sides of the same coin," suggesting that disproportionate discipline was a key contributor to disproportionate academic achievement (Gregory, Skiba, Noguera, 2010). They cited several bodies of literature linking the two gaps such as lost instructional time due to suspension and expulsion and school pushout, and this body of literature has only continued to grow:

- Arcia (2006): Two cohorts of students were matched on demographics and academics with one group experiencing a single suspension and the other no suspensions. The students experiencing a single suspension were three grade levels behind the other students after just one year, and nearly five grade levels behind after the second year.

- Safer (1986): Low academic achievement and low IQ best predicted if a student would be left back in elementary school, but in junior high school the best predictors were behavioral suspensions and absenteeism.

- Morris and Perry (2016): School suspensions accounted for one-fifth of the differences between Black and White students' school performance even after accounting for social, demographic, and family structure differences.

- Kelly (2010): Teachers in primarily African American schools were more likely to report problem behaviors, which created a disruption-mitigating culture that resulted in less interactive discourse and more seat work.

- Skiba and Rausch (2004): In Indiana alone, the schools with the highest use of out-of-school suspension on average had 48% of students passing standardized test while in the lowest 25% of out-of-school suspension use 62% of students passed the state assessments.

While none of these studies conclusively demonstrate that academic achievement differences stem from implicit bias-driven effects on school discipline, they establish a clear link between school discipline discrepancies and academic discrepancies. In this way, implicit bias becomes a double-edged sword shown in Figure 3.6 that cuts through school equity no matter which direction it swings.

The next chapter will discuss the impacts of implicit bias on school discipline to clarify the second edge of this sword. With the combination of implicit-bias related challenges stemming from both academic and disciplinary interferences, the "tip of the sword" reflects the school-to-prison pipeline (see Chapter 1) that carries these detriments throughout the students' lives into their lives as adults. As you can see, implicit bias in schools may have impacts that appear to affect students in the short term, but compounded these challenges create the platform necessary to perpetuate this pipeline. Read on considering your own experiences at both ends of implicit bias: as a doer and receiver. While much research has been done on implicit bias in schools, only through self-reflection and application can we really internalize the meaning of such bias in our roles as educators and leaders.

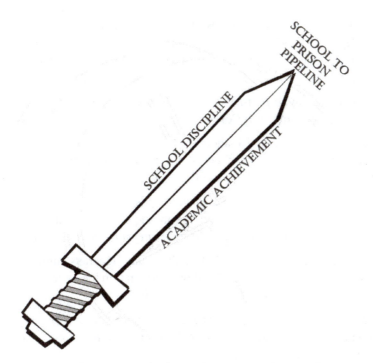

Figure 3.6 The double-edged sword of implicit bias works to act on students through academic achievement and school discipline during school years, but extends through life by means of the school-to-prison pipeline

References

Arcia, E. (2006). Achievement and enrollment status of suspended students: Outcomes in a large, multicultural school district. *Education and Urban Society*, *38*(3), 359–369.

Boysen, G. A., & Vogel, D. L. (2009). Bias in the classroom: Types, frequencies, and responses. *Teaching of Psychology*, *36*(1), 12–17.

Capers, Q. I., Clinchot, D., McDougle, L., & Greenwald, A. G. (2017). Implicit racial bias in medical school admissions. *Academic Medicine*, *92*(3), 365–369.

Dee, T. S. (2004). Teachers, race, and student achievement in a randomized experiment. *The Review of Economics and Statistics*, *86*(1), 195–210.

Ferguson, R. F. (2003). Teachers' perceptions and expectations and the Black-White test score gap. *Urban Education*, *38*(4), 460–507.

Friedrich, A., Flunger, B., Nagengast, B., Jonkmann, K., & Trautwein, U. (2015). Pygmalion effects in the classroom: Teacher expectancy effects on students' math achievement. *Contemporary Educational Psychology, 41*, 1–12.

Gay, G. (2010). *Culturally responsive teaching: Theory, research, and practice* (2nd ed.). New York, NY: Corwin Press.

Gershenson, S., Holt, S. B., & Papageorge, N. (2016). Who believes in me? The effect of student-teacher demographic match on teacher expectations. *Economics of Education Review, 52*, 209–224.

Glock, S., & Klapproth, F. (2017). Bad boys, good girls? Implicit and explicit attitudes toward ethnic minority students among elementary and secondary school teachers. *Studies in Educational Evaluation, 53*, 77–86.

Glock, S., Kneer, J., & Kovacs, C. (2013). Preservice teachers' implicit attitudes toward students with and without immigration background: A pilot study. *Studies in Educational Evaluation, 39*, 204–210.

Goings, R. B., & Ford, D. Y. (2018). Investigating the intersection of poverty and race in gifted education journals: A 15-year analysis. *Gifted Child Quarterly, 62*(1), 25–36.

Gregory, A., Skiba, R. J., & Noguera, P. A. (2010). The achievement gap and the discipline gap: Two sides of the same coin? *Educational Researcher, 39*(1), 59–68.

Griner, A. C., & Stewart, M. L. (2013). Addressing the achievement gap and disproportionality through the use of culturally responsive teaching practices. *Urban Education, 48*(4), 585–621.

Grissom, J. A., & Redding, C. (2015). Discretion and disproportionality: Explaining the underrepresentation of high-achieving students of color in gifted programs. *Aera Open, 2*(1). https://doi.org/10.1177/2332858415622175

Jacoby-Senghor, D. S., Sinclair, S., & Shelton, J. N. (2016). A lesson in bias: The relationship between implicit racial bias and performance in pedagogical contexts. *Journal of Experimental Social Psychology, 63*, 50–55.

Jussim, L., & Eccles, J. S. (1992). Teacher expectations: II. Construction and reflection of student achievement. *Journal of Personality and Social Psychology, 63*(6), 947–961.

Jussim, L., Eccles, J., & Madon, S. (1996). Social perception, social stereotypes, and teacher expectations: Accuracy and the quest for the powerful self-fulfilling prophecy. *Advances in Experimental Social Psychology, 28*, 281–388.

Kelly, S. (2010). A crisis in authority in predominantly Black schools. *Teachers College Record, 112*(5), 1247–1274.

Khalifa, M. A., Gooden, M. A., & Davis, J. D. (2016). Culturally responsive school leadership: A synthesis of the literature. *Review of Educational Research, 86*(4), 1272–1311.

Kumar, R., Karabenick, S. A., & Burgoon, J. N. (2015). Teachers' implicit attitudes, explicit beliefs, and the mediating role of respect and cultural responsibility on mastery and performance-focused instructional practices. *Journal of Educational Psychology, 107*(2), 533–545.

Logan, J. R., & Burdick-Will, J. (2016). School segregation, charter schools, and access to quality education. *Journal of Urban Affairs, 38*(3), 323–343.

Magee, S.-K. (2015). College admissions essays: A genre of masculinity. *Young Scholars In Writing, 7*, 116–121.

McKown, C., & Weinstein, R. S. (2008). Teacher expectations, classroom context, and the achievement gap. *Journal of School Psychology, 46*(3), 235–261.

Milkman, K. L., Akinola, M., & Chugh, D. (2015). What happens before? A field experiment exploring how pay and representation differentially shape bias on the pathway into organizations. *Journal of Applied Psychology, 100*(6), 1678–1712.

Morris, E. W., & Perry, B. L. (2016). The punishment gap: School suspension and racial disparities in achievement. *Social Problems, 63*(1), 68–86.

Peterson, E., Rubie-Davies, C., Osborne, D., & Sibley, C. (2016). Teachers' explicit expectations and implicit prejudiced attitudes to educational achievement: Relations with student achievement and the ethnic achievement gap. *Learning and Instruction, 42*, 123–140.

Reschly, D. J. (1997). *Disproportionate minority representation in general and special education: Patterns, issues, and alternatives*. Des Moines, IA: Mountain Plains Regional Resources Center, Drake University.

Rist, R. C. (2000). Student social class and teacher expectations: The self-fulfilling prophecy in ghetto education. *Harvard Educational Review, 70*(3), 257–301.

Ross, S. I., & Jackson, J. M. (1991). Teachers' expectations for Black males' and Black females' academic achievement. *Personality and Social Psychology Bulletin, 17*(1), 78–82.

Safer, D. J. (1986). Nonpromotion correlates and outcomes at different grade levels. *Journal of Learning Disabilities, 19*(8), 500–503.

Skiba, R. J., & Rausch, M. K. (2004). *The relationship between achievement, discipline, and race: An analysis of factors predicting ISTEP scores* (Children Left Behind Policy Briefs) (pp. 1–5). Bloomington, IN: Center for Evaluation and Education Policy, Indiana University.

Taylor, M. C. (1979). Race, sex, and the expression of self-fulfilling prophecies in a laboratory teaching situation. *Journal of Personality and Social Psychology, 37*(6), 897–912.

Tenebaum, H. R., & Ruck, M. D. (2007). Are teachers' expectations different for racial minority than for European American students? A meta-analysis. *Journal of Educational Psychology, 99*(2), 253–273.

Van den Bergh, L., Denessen, E., Hornstra, L., Voeten, M., & Holland, R. W. (2010). The implicit prejudiced attitudes of teachers: Relations to teacher expectations and the ethnic achievement gap. *American Educational Research Journal, 47*(2), 497–527.

Woolley, M. E., Strutchens, M. E., Gilbert, M. C., & Martin, W. G. (2010). Mathematics success of Black middle school students: Direct and indirect effects of teacher expectations and reform practices. *Negro Educational Review, 61*(1–4), 41–59, 123–124.

Yull, A. (2015). The impact of race and socioeconomic status on access to accommodations in postsecondary education. *Journal of Gender, Social Policy, and the Law, 23*(2), 353–392.

Who Did What?
Behavior and Discipline

Introduction

As the bell rang, Jeffrey ran down the hall and into Mr. Price's classroom just a minute or two late. He was always worried he'd get caught – he knew he was late more often than he was on time – but his locker was all the way down the hall! Right behind him, Lakeisha hurried into the room holding more books than she could really handle. She was a good student, but Jeffrey knew she was always getting into trouble. He shouted to Mr. Price, "Hey, look who's finally here!" Mr. Price peered over and saw the two coming into the classroom and immediately scolded Lakeisha for having too many books: "You get locker time between every other class; what do you need all those books for right now?" Lakeisha tried to explain that her locker was three floors down, and she didn't want to be late for her other classes on this floor today, but Mr. Price stopped her: "So, it's OK to be late for *my* class? Is American Literature a joke to you, young lady?" Jeffrey mumbled to his friends: "If we have to read about more pregnant ladies and pilgrims, it can't really be serious, right?" Standing beside the group, Mr. Price commented that at least the boys knew what *The Scarlet Letter* was about. Lakeisha always did her reading and tried to tell Mr. Price that, but Mr. Price sent her into the hall for talking back and to the office with a referral for tardiness and insubordination. "Jeffrey, try to get here on time, son. Now open your books to page 123, class."

As you read the story above, how did you picture the class? Were most students White? Black? Latinx? How much of the class was male or female? What race/ethnicity was Mr. Price, Jeffrey, Lakeisha? What did the school and classroom look like? How were the students and teachers dressed? As you think about all these questions, you might begin to see how a story trying to make you think of bias in discipline reveals many other implicit biases you might hold yourself. Even educators focused on combating the effects of implicit bias and working toward equity typically view Lakeisha as Black and Mr. Price and Jeffrey as White. When studying implicit bias, many researchers use vignettes similar to this to reveal implicit biases. Consider the following vignette:

> *Josh is a B student in your sixth grade science class who is popular with many of the girls and a key player on the soccer team. While on cafeteria duty, you see Josh pinch one of the more popular seventh grade girls, Melissa. She smacks his hand and glares at him, but her friends send Josh away before returning to talk with Melissa.*

What, if anything, would you do? How may this change if you exchange Josh for Jamal? What if you change Melissa for Mercedes? While we rarely want to admit to bias, our gut reactions tend to change based on peoples' races – especially when linked to behavior expectations. Moreover, one of the complexities of discipline is that it often centers on a series of ambiguities that activate implicit biases. How do you know when to give a student a warning or suspend them when behaviors and motives are unclear? In the legal system, we allow for a jury of one's peers to decide, but in schools such decisions are often unilateral. Layering the effects of implicit bias on the challenge of discipline decisions does not make decisions any easier.

Defining discipline is not always easy, but researchers typically measure discipline using office disciplinary referrals (ODRs) or discipline outcomes such as suspensions or expulsions. Both measures relate to discipline and students, but neither is a perfect measure. While ODRs fail to account for incidents of discipline that were contained in the classroom environment, discipline outcomes misrepresent incidents with multiple responses. For example, after Joey writes on the classroom wall, Ms. Sora has him wash off the wall and makes no ODR. When Joey writes on the classroom wall in Ms. Wilkes class, he is sent to the office resulting in two lunch detentions and the task of washing the wall. In only the latter instance would an ODR be reported, and in that same instance the outcome could be categorized as either a corrective action or a detention. To further confound this, Joey's school might only record ODRs resulting in at least a suspension in their data collection system, thereby making the incident invisible to most researchers. This understanding is important when considering findings related to discipline because so much discipline goes unreported in studies, leading to lower estimates of impact and smaller racial discrepancies.

Kelly Hurst (2016), a school administrator, wrote about racial inequity in her school by recounting an incident when a teacher made a big deal and ODR about a Black student wearing sagging pants (a dress code violation). While walking the student to the office, Hurst noticed four White boys in sagging pants that went completely unnoticed by teachers. When she commented loudly to one of these boys, a nearby teacher told the student to pull up his pants. The Black student could have received the same treatment, but didn't. How does this come across in the data we see in studies? It doesn't. Either a study will show that one population experiences ODRs so many times more often than another, or it will discuss discrepancies in the outcomes. While experiencing an ODR starts to get at the issue, it fails to account for the fact that all five boys exhibited the same behavior. As you can see, discipline studies are not perfect and tend to soften the discrepancies in discipline by race due to imperfect data.

Despite this challenge, research focusing on disproportionalities tend to use the same indicators but compare them to the overall population of students. If 20 out of 80 Black students and 30 out of 60 White students got high-fives from the principal, 25% of Black students and 50% of White students received high-fives. The discrepancy here would be 25%, but the difference is only 10 high-fives. One study might say that White students receive high-fives 150% more often than Black students based on the counted values (20 × 1.50 = 30), but another could say White students received high-fives 200% more often than Black students based on the proportions (25 × 2.00 = 50). Because proportions account for the representation of students in the population of the school, district, country, or other appropriate group, these results often provide the most impactful results. Going forward, note whether the number/count or proportion is reported to best understand the impact.

Exclusionary Discipline

Discipline outcomes can be inclusionary (no lost instruction) or exclusionary (lost instruction). Inclusionary discipline includes outcomes like corrective actions, detentions, conferences, and schedule adjustments; exclusionary discipline includes outcomes like suspensions, expulsions, arrests, and alternative educational placements. While overuse of any discipline outcome has the potential to be harmful, exclusionary discipline has been associated with academic decline (Perry, & Morris, 2014), high school dropout (Balfanz, Byrnes, & Fox, 2014), grade retention (Marchbanks et al., 2015), and delinquency (Rosenbaum, 2018). A classic review of the detrimental effects associated with suspensions noted that suspensions:

> (1) take away educational time that may cause marginal, weak, or poorly motivated students to drop out permanently; (2) label children as "troublemakers" thereby making repeated behavior problems more likely; (3) deny children needed help; and (4) contribute to juvenile delinquency by putting unsupervised children and those with problems into the streets.
>
> (Children's Defense Fund, 1975, p. 62)

As such, much research focused on the disciplinary over-representation of students of Color is centered around exclusionary discipline or specific exclusionary outcomes.

The Big Deal: The Punishment/School Discipline Gap

While exclusionary discipline is a concern for all students, we focus here on the discrepancy by race (and some focus on gender) due to the sizable school discipline gap. Data reported for the 2013–2014 school year to the U.S. Department of Education's Office of Civil Rights Data Collection found that while only about 15% of all K-12 U.S. public school students identified as African American or Black, these students made up 30–40% of those receiving in-school suspensions, out-of-school suspensions, and expulsions. One might begin by assuming that this is indicative of Black students misbehaving more often or more severely, but studies show that

Black students not only behave similarly to White students, but also tend to receive more severe discipline and are referred to the office more often for the same behaviors as White students (see Anyon et al., 2014; Huang, 2018). This gap also exists at a lesser extent for Hispanic students who again behave similar to their peers (Welch & Payne, 2018). Race discrepancies in discipline despite similar behavior raise school equity concerns, but also highlight the possible impact of implicit bias and potential of related interventions.

Going back to our discipline discrepancy calculations, Black students were over-represented by up to 25% for exclusionary discipline types, while White students were under-represented by up to 17% (ranges are used because each exclusionary discipline type is measured separately; actual numbers can be explored on the Civil Rights Data Collection website).

The Influence of Implicit Bias on Discipline Decisions

When Implicit Bias Slips In

Behavioral decisions are not always open to bias. Objective decisions offer decision-makers clear paths to results, such as a red light always meaning you should stop the car. But what happens when you approach a yellow light? Do you speed up to get through, proceed with caution per policy, slow down, or stop to be cautious? Just like the ambiguity of a yellow traffic light brings uncertainty, so do more subjective disciplinary infractions – and such decisions become what Kent McIntosh refers to as "vulnerable decision points" where ambiguity can increase the impact of implicit bias (McIntosh, Girvan, Horner, & Smolkowski, 2014). Research shows that Black students are most often sent to the office for subjective offenses such as threat, excessive noise, and loitering rather than objective offenses such as fighting, carrying a weapon, or smoking (Bradshaw, Mitchell, O'Brennan, & Leaf, 2010; Skiba, Michael, Nardo, & Peterson, 2002). Even when Black and White students are sent to the office at similar rates, referrals for Black students typically stem from less severe and more discretionary offenses than those of White students (Fabelo et al., 2011; Kelly, 2010). In fact, differences in the amount of subjective ODRs experienced by Black and White students almost completely accounted for the differences in exclusionary discipline disproportionalities in one study (Girvan, Gion, McIntosh, & Smolkowski, 2016). While objectivity may remain the goal, the complexities of discipline can create challenges. One principal stated:

> I guess I can't help but be a little subjective… it's different if you've built a relationship with the kid versus not having built one. They're easier to approach and almost easier to reprimand. I really don't believe it's human nature to be objective.
>
> (Kennedy, Murphy, & Jordan, 2017, p. 261)

Another challenge to objectivity is the ambiguous nature of the discipline infractions themselves. For example, one school leader's sense of "disruptive behavior" or "excessive noise" may not align with that of a colleague. These ambiguous situations can lead to the emergence of implicit bias, as "social psychology research suggests that implicit racial biases are most likely to affect decision making when the decision involves an ambiguous situation and provides the biased decision maker some ground to justify the biased decision on nonracial grounds" (Simson, 2014, p. 545). Stated more simply: the lack of clarity in subjective decisions provides an alternative to race-based explanations of biased behaviors, making implicit bias more likely to interfere in these decisions. As such, school leaders need to be mindful of moments of ambiguity and recognize that implicit biases may be playing a role in how subjective situations are perceived.

Teacher-Level Impact

Most research directly linking school discipline with implicit bias focuses on teacher–student classroom interactions. These studies typically use indirect measures of implicit bias such as racial mismatch between the teacher and student (e.g., a Black student with a White teacher) or vignettes that differ only by the student's name using traditionally African American names such as Jamal and Latoya versus common Caucasian American names including Josh and Emma. In 2015, one researcher used a very large data set (Early Childhood Longitudinal Study or ECLS) to look at implicit bias and discipline through racial mismatch (Wright, 2015). This study compared the teacher–student interactions experienced by students across all the teachers each student encountered throughout the school day. Findings indicated that White teachers reported behavior problems by Black males much more than Black teachers (no difference by teacher gender). In this study, racial mismatch only significantly related to the experience of Black males and not to the experiences of White or Hispanic students or female students. Interestingly, the effects seen for these Black male students were temporary and did not continue once the student moved into the next grade and no longer interacted with the prior racially mismatched teacher. This suggests that the effect was specific to the teacher–student relationship present in that classroom and potentially indicates teacher bias (either explicit or implicit). Moreover, the researchers in this study went on to link the higher incidences of reported behavior problems to equally higher suspension rates for those Black male students and suggested that by simply doubling students' exposure to same-race teachers, discipline gaps might be as much as halved.

Another 2015 study used the vignette method to evaluate differences in behavior reporting and disciplinary outcome perspectives (Okonofua & Eberhardt, 2015). Racially diverse, female teachers were told to imagine themselves as teachers in a middle school as they read through the disciplinary record of either Darnell, Deshawn, Greg, or Jake. The identical records each included two infractions with a brief description of each: insubordination and class disturbance. After reading and answering some basic self-demographics, teachers rated the severity of the behavior, interference the behavior would cause, and the irritation provoked by the behavior to provide a "feeling trouble" rating. They also rated the severity of the appropriate punishment and whether they considered the student a "troublemaker."

The teachers were significantly more likely to consider the student a troublemaker when the traditionally African American names were used in the vignette, and this label accounted for differences in how severe the teachers thought the student should be punished. These disturbing findings led the researchers to then triple the amount of participating teachers and specifically ask if the teachers thought the behaviors were indicative of a pattern and whether the teacher would suspend the student. The same relationship was found this time with both the troublemaker label and the indication of a behavioral pattern underlying the relationship between race and discipline severity and the relationship between race and suspension. In fact, when teachers were asked about whether behaviors were indicative of a larger pattern of misbehavior after only one of the two behavioral incidents, they were more likely to note such patterns in the students with traditionally African American names – especially in the case of applying a troublemaker label.

While both these studies indicated differences in teacher discipline by race, neither displayed teachers that appeared to be intentionally discriminating against students. Jason Nance (2016) wrote:

> Because most teachers and school administrators seem to be acting in good faith and there is substantial evidence that minority students are not misbehaving at higher rates than similarly situated white students, logically we can attribute at least some of these disparities to the unconscious biases of educators.
>
> (Nance, 2016, p. 1073)

Implicit bias works to create an uneven playing field with regards to student discipline by race, which is unfortunately present even before kindergarten.

In 2016, a study of preschool teachers began exploring the implicit bias-specific elements of disciplinary discrimination by race using eye tracking and self-reported data in conjunction with the vignette approach (Gilliam, Maupin, Reyes, Accavitti, & Shic, 2016). During the study teachers were asked to watch a video of four students (Black female, Black male, White female, White male) playing and to press a button any time they saw a problem behavior (although none occurred). Eye-tracking software measured the amount of time the teachers looked at each student, and teachers were asked to rank who they thought they had to look at most often. Teachers in the study spent the most time looking at Black students, especially the Black boy, with Black teachers spending even more time looking at Black students than White teachers. Interestingly, 42% of teachers responded that the Black boy required the most of their attention, followed by 32% reporting the White boy, 13% the White girl, and 10% the Black girl. In this scenario, teachers appeared aware of a tendency to be more critical of behaviors in the Black boy, but not for Black students overall. The study continued with a vignette detailing a behavior incident with or without background information about the child's home environment. In this instance, teachers rated the severity of the behavior, degree

Table 4.1 Behavior Severity by Racial (Mis)Match With and Without Background Information

Teacher Race	Student Race	Without Background Information	With Background Information
Black	Black	+	−
	White	−	+
White	Black	−	=
	White	+	=

Note: Severity rankings are indicated with a + for more severe, − for less severe, or = for equal severity as compared to the comparison student race.

of hopelessness for improving the behavior of that child, and whether and for how long they would recommend the child be suspended from school. Contrary to other findings, the preschool teachers showed no differences in whether and how long they would suspend Black or White students, but Black teachers tended to recommend longer suspensions overall. There were interesting findings as to how teachers ranked the severity of the students' behaviors, as shown in Table 4.1.

Statistically taken a step further, the researchers found that when teachers and students were racially matched, teacher behavior severity rankings tended to decrease with the addition of background information and when unmatched, ratings increased. In other words, knowing more about the student's situation only helped if the teacher and student were of the same race, and actually hurt when they were not of the same race. The participating teachers may have been more or less critical of students of matched races prior to knowing background information based on expected backgrounds; those with background information seemed to have differential empathies with students based on racial match. These results indicate that implicit bias begins in preschool and works on perceptions of behavior and expectations for bad behavior rather than through differences in ideas about the actual punishment of students. Students of Color are referred for discipline at higher rates leading to discrepant levels of discipline, but the teachers' involvement in the discipline choices does not appear to drive discrepancies in exclusionary versus inclusionary discipline – at least in early education. If discrepancies in the kind of discipline students receive is not entirely driven by teachers, then implicit bias is implicated at the disciplinary decision maker's level as well.

Administrator-Level Impact

Various schools approach discipline outcome judgements differently using principals, vice/assistant principals, deans, and other administrators to determine the appropriate corrective action for a behavior infraction. Here, we refer to administrators as any person involved in the final determination of a disciplinary outcome to overcome that variability in specific titles for these critical decision-makers. While we know that ODRs account for at least some of the differences in subjective discipline by race and perhaps all of the differences by gender from research (Skiba et al., 2002), the portion of differences in subjective discipline that is not explained and potentially most differences in objective discipline seem related to school-level factors (Skiba, Chung, Trachok, Baker, Sheya, & Hughes, 2014). While many school-level factors related to objective discipline might stem from systemic racism and policy, subjective discipline discrepancies may stem from administrator bias (Brown, 2017; Gullo, 2017).

Although little work has explored implicit bias in school administrators, one study measured the implicit bias of school administrators using the Implicit Association Test and paired administrators' implicit bias level to behavioral incidents for which that administrator was the primary discipline decision-maker (Gullo, 2017). After taking into consideration the severity of the behavior infraction and student factors such as free lunch eligibility, administrators' implicit bias accounted for nearly all of the differences in subjective discipline severity by race that occurred between different administrators. In other words, administrator implicit bias explained why one administrator tended to give students of Color more or less severe discipline (suspension versus a detention) as compared to a different administrator. Interestingly, administrators' implicit bias was completely unrelated to racial differences in discipline severity for objective decisions (although there were still differences in discipline severity by race in those objective disciplinary decisions). This indicates that implicit bias in school administrators might explain the remaining discipline differences by race once differences stemming from the classroom are already considered.

But Why?

Even though it is easy to attribute differences in discipline by race and gender to implicit bias, it often doesn't satisfy our drive to really understand our actions. Much of our bias-driven behavior stems from these automatic stereotypes due to the unconscious or "in-the-moment" nature of these kinds of decisions, but sometimes we experience more explicit biases driven by implicit bias. Amanda Lewis and John Diamond discuss a case study of Riverview High School in their book, *Despite the Best Intentions: How Racial Inequality Thrives in Good Schools* (2015). Over and over again there are accounts of bias in action: less severe punishment of White students due to the higher potential to sue, parents requesting White students get a break because they deserve one, the choice to name one behavior horse-play and another inappropriate conduct. The difference in this book is that the students' perceptions are included and discussed. While the students rarely suggest that the teachers are being "racist," they recognize differential treatment. Some actions might occur as microaggressions where behaviors are differentiated for reasons that seem legitimate for a reason outside of race, but really reflect discriminatory actions based on race. Together, implicit bias and explicit bias created a culture where best intentions at Riverview High School resulted in racial inequity that is not very different from most schools.

Microaggressions are subtle indignities that serve as an indirect form of discrimination. Comprising of either actions or words, they are not necessarily meant to be malicious but nevertheless can insult the recipient based on attributes such as his or her race, gender, nationality, ability status, religion, etc. Examples include:

- Consistently mispronouncing a student's name rather than taking the time to learn how to say it properly.
- Assuming an Asian student will not need further assistance with a geometry assignment because "All Asians are good at math."
- Asking a student to speak in a class discussion in such a manner that they are seen as representing their larger race, ethnicity, gender, etc.
- Consistently using examples or assigning readings that only reinforce traditional gender roles.

Microaggressions can be intentional or unintentional, but regardless of intent, their hostile or derogative nature yields a subtle harm that, particularly when experienced cumulatively over time, can weigh negatively on the recipient.

Implicit Microaggressions

The school I worked for provided bi-monthly "cultural sensitivity" trainings to teachers regarding students of "every" background (i.e., Latino, African American, special needs) but never the needs of the Muslim students. Unfortunately, this one training made teachers incapable of meeting students' cultural needs. For example, teachers routinely provided young Muslim students with snacks containing gelatin (which Muslims cannot consume because it is a pork product) without their parents' knowledge. Teachers did not know the names of various clothing pieces worn by Muslim students (i.e., "hijab," "kufi") and routinely called them by the wrong names, which led to confusion among younger students and resentment among the older ones. Even after several teachers voiced concerns over sensitive topics included in the curriculum, parents were never invited into the curricular discussion or even notified that potentially counter-religious topic were part of the curriculum.

– Anna Danylyuk

Fortunately, the task of addressing these racial inequities is far from impossible. Part III of this book is devoted to providing strategies at the individual and institutional levels that help overcome the barriers to school equity created by implicit bias. When a child accidentally spills the milk, we teach her to hold a cup with two hands. Similarly, we can learn to use strategies to avoid racial inequities driven unintentionally by our biases. The ability to quell the impact of implicit bias is core to the importance of recognizing how and when implicit biases affect our students.

References

Anyon, Y., Jenson, J. M., Altschul, I., Farrar, J., McQueen, J., Freer, E., ... Simmons, J. (2014). The persistent effect of race and the promise of alternatives to suspension in school discipline outcomes. *Children and Youth Services Review, 44,* 379–386.

Balfanz, R., Byrnes, V., & Fox, J. (2014). Sent home and put off-track: The antecedents, disproportionalities, and consequences of being suspended in the ninth grade. *Journal of Applied Research on Children:*

Informing Policy for Children at Risk, 5(2), Article 13. Retrieved from http://digitalcommons.library.tmc.edu/cgi/viewcontent.cgi?article=12 17&context=childrenatrisk

Bradshaw, C. P., Mitchell, M. M., O'Brennan, L. M., & Leaf, P. J. (2010). Multilevel exploration of factors contributing to the overrepresentation of Black students in office disciplinary referrals. *Journal of Educational Psychology, 102,* 508–520.

Brown, A. L. (2017). From subhuman to human kind: Implicit bias, racial memory, and Black males in schools and society. *Peabody Journal of Education, 93*(1), 52–65. https://doi.org/10.1080/0161956X. 2017.1403176

Children's Defense Fund. (1975). *School suspensions: Are they helping children?* Cambridge, MA: Washington Research Project.

Fabelo, T., Thompson, M. D., Plotkin, M., Carmichael, D., Marchbanks, M. P., & Booth, E. A. (2011). *Breaking school rules: A statewide study of how school discipline relates to students' success and juvenile justice involvement.* New York, NY: Council of State Governments Justice Center. Retrieved from www.edweek.org/media/breakingschoolsrules-37story.pdf

Gilliam, W. S., Maupin, A. N., Reyes, C. R., Accavitti, M., & Shic, F. (2016). *Do early educators' implicit biases regarding sex and race relate to behavior expectations and recommendations of preschool expulsions and suspensions?* Yale University Child Study Center. Retrieved from https://medicine.yale.edu/childstudy/zigler/publications/Preschool% 20Implicit%20Bias%20Policy%20Brief_final_9_26_276766_5379_ v1.pdf

Girvin, E. J., Gion, C., McIntosh, K., & Smolkowski, K. (2016). The relative contribution of subjective office referrals to racial disproportionality in school discipline. *School Psychology Quarterly, 32*(3), 392–404.

Gullo, G. L. (2017). *Administrator implicit bias in school disciplinary decisions* (Doctoral Dissertation). Lehigh University, Bethlehem, PA. Retrieved from https://preserve.lehigh.edu/cgi/viewcontent.cgi?article= 3617&context=etd

Huang, F. L. (2018). Do Black students misbehave more? Investigating the differential involvement hypothesis and out-of-school suspensions. *The Journal of Educational Research, 111*(3), 284–294. https://doi.org/ 10.1080/00220671.2016.1253538

Hurst, K. W. (2016, December 7). Biased discipline at my school. *Edutopia*. Retrieved from www.edutopia.org/article/biased-discipline-at-my-school-kelly-wickham-hurst

Kelly, S. (2010). A crisis in authority in predominantly Black schools. *Teachers College Record, 112*(5), 1247–1274.

Kennedy, B. L., Murphy, A. S., & Jordan, A. (2017). Title I middle school administrators' beliefs and choices about using corporal punishment and exclusionary discipline. *American Journal of Education, 123*(2), 243–280.

Lewis, A., & Diamond, J. (2015). *Despite the best intentions: How racial inequality thrives in good schools*. New York, NY: Oxford University Press.

Marchbanks, M. P., Blake, J. J., Booth, E. A., Carmichael, D., Seibert, A. L., & Fabelo, T. (2015). The economic effects of exclusionary discipline on grade retention and high school dropout. In D. Losen (Ed.), *Closing the school discipline gap: Equitable remedies for excessive exclusion* (pp. 59–74). New York, NY: Teachers College Press.

McIntosh, K., Girvan, E. J., Horner, R., & Smolkowski, K. (2014). Education not incarceration: A conceptual model of reducing racial and ethnic disproportionality in school discipline. *Journal of Applied Research on Children*, 5(2), Article 4.

Nance, J. P. (2016). *Over-disciplining students, racial bias, and the school-to-prison pipeline*. University of Florida Law Scholarship Repository. Retrieved from http://scholarship.law.ufl.edu/cgi/viewcontent.cgi?article=1766&context=facultypub

Office of Civil Rights. (2014). *Civil rights data collection: Data snapshot (school discipline)*. Washington, DC: US Department of Education Office for Civil Rights. Retrieved from www2.ed.gov/about/offices/list/ocr/docs/crdc-discipline-snapshot.pdf

Okonofua, J. A., & Eberhardt, J. L. (2015). Two strikes: Race and the disciplining of young students. *Psychological Science, 26*(5), 617–624.

Perry, B. L., & Morris, E. W. (2014). Suspending progress: Collateral consequences of exclusionary punishment in public schools. *American Sociological Review, 79*(6), 1067–1087.

Rosenbaum, J. (2018). Educational and criminal justice outcomes 12 years after school suspension. *Youth & Society*. https://doi.org/10.1177/0044118X17752208

Simson, D. (2014). Exclusion, punishment, racism, and our schools: A critical race theory perspective on school discipline. *UCLA Law Review, 62*(3), 506–565.

Skiba, R. J., Chung, C. G., Trachok, M., Baker, T. L., Sheya, A., & Hughes, R. L. (2014). Parsing disciplinary disproportionality: Contribution of infraction, student, and school characteristics to out-of-school suspension and expulsion. *American Educational Research Journal, 51*(4), 640–670.

Skiba, R. J., Michael, R. S., Nardo, A. C., & Peterson, R. L. (2002). The color of discipline: Sources of racial and gender disproportionality in school punishment. *The Urban Review, 34*(4), 317–342.

Welch, K., & Payne, A. A. (2018). Latino/a student threat and school disciplinary policies and practices. *Sociology of Education, 91*(2), 91–110. https://doi.org/10.1177/0038040718757720

Wright, A. C. (2015). *Teachers' perceptions of students' disruptive behavior: The effect of racial congruence and consequences for school suspension* (Unpublished Manuscript). Santa Barbara, CA: University of California Department of Economics. Retrieved from https://aefpweb.org/sites/default/files/webform/41/Race%20Match,%20Disruptive%20Behavior,%20and%20School%20Suspension.pdf

What Can We Do about Implicit Bias?

Making a Difference by Yourself
Individual Strategies

Introduction

Now that you are aware of some of the real-world effects that implicit bias can create in your school, the next step is to do something about it! Knowing that we all can behave based on perceptions and associations that are outside our conscious awareness can be a little unsettling at first. In some ways, it can feel like we are unable to control our own actions. However, it's important to realize that our unconscious associations have no bearing on our conscious values; good people have biases too! Yet, if we do nothing to interrupt implicit bias, our good intentions and unconscious behaviors will continue to be at odds. An understanding of implicit bias can help all of us align our intentions and actions to create more equitable and inclusive schools. Fortunately, there are several interventions that can reduce the negative effects of bias.

In this chapter, we'll discuss four research-based interventions: (1) decision-making supports, (2) intergroup contact, (3) mindfulness, and (4) counter-stereotypic exemplars. In total, these interventions have shown success in not only interrupting our implicit biases from having an influence over our behavior, but also re-wiring the associations that we've formed. This chapter will discuss each of these interventions in depth and explain how they work to combat the effects of implicit bias. We conclude with some practical strategies for reducing implicit bias by incorporating these approaches into your personal and professional practice.

Decision-Making Supports

Have you ever made a decision you regretted simply because you were stressed out, exhausted, or hungry? Of course! We have all been there! Even if we can be rational decision-makers at times, we all regularly encounter a variety of circumstances and difficult decisions that diminish our ability to be objective and fair. Decision-making supports are simply steps you can take to buffer the negative effects of cognitive load (i.e., stress, metal fatigue). There is no one right way to create mental space and capacity; thus, decision supports can include a number of tactics, including: taking a break, asking for someone else's opinion, or simply taking time to reflect on your own ability to be objective as a means to slow down and regain your ability to make more logical decisions. For example, if you are feeling hungry, waiting until after lunch to make important decisions can even be beneficial. Similarly, taking a 10-minute break can sometimes help improve productivity to a much greater extent than just trying to power through the moment.

As we discussed in previous chapters, people are more susceptible to the influence of implicit bias when their decision-making ability is constrained by other factors, such as having to get a lot of things done in a small amount of time, multitasking, or making decisions based on subjective or unclear information (Van Ryn & Saha, 2011). As educational leaders, making difficult decisions and navigating stressful situations are an everyday occurrence. Of course, it is not possible to wave a magic wand and make these stressors disappear. Instead, embracing decision-making supports can encourage you to make the best of your decision-making abilities in the moments where conscious control may be the most limited. By taking breaks and employing additional decision supports, we can reduce our chances of slipping into autopilot and defaulting to our unconscious processing.

Intergroup Contact

We have a natural proclivity to associate with and relate to people who are similar to ourselves – whether that be similar backgrounds, experiences, or identities (Allport, 1954; Brewer, 1999). Although this tendency is not inherently bad, it may keep us from looking beyond our comfort zones and building meaningful relationships with diverse groups of people. Conversely, intergroup contact is the intentional exposure to groups of people outside of our regular social circles.

The concept of intergroup contact emerged in the 1950s through the work of Gordon Allport, a Harvard psychologist, whose research was one of the first to explore the social and psychological underpinnings of racial prejudice (Allport, 1954). Allport's work revealed that interacting with diverse groups of people is one of the most effective ways to reduce prejudice, stereotyping, and intergroup conflict. Contemporary research illustrates that intergroup contact is not only an effective method for reducing *explicit* prejudice and bias, but having meaningful interactions with diverse groups of people can combat implicit bias toward a variety of identities (Dasgupta, 2013; Kubota, Peiso, Marcum, & Cloutier, 2017; Pettigrew & Tropp, 2006; Vezzali & Giovannini, 2011). Developing meaningful relationships helps us develop empathy and see people as individuals rather than a representation of a larger social group or identity.

Allport's Intergroup Contact Theory offers five conditions where contact across social groups is most effective: (1) when groups have equal social standing or status, (2) when both groups are working toward a common goal or purpose, (3) when the process for achieving the goal(s) is collaborative rather than competitive or coercive, (4) when intergroup contact is mutually supported by laws, institutional norms, or authority figures, and (5) when interactions are personal and informal (Allport, 1954). While these conditions are ideal, modern findings suggest only two conditions are really necessary for intergroup contact to have beneficial effects: empathy and reduced anxiety (Pettigrew, Tropp, Wagner, & Christ, 2011). As long as you are sure to make intergroup contact under low-anxiety conditions where you are able to have empathy toward others, this strategy can be effective.

Mindfulness

In the United States, busyness and high productivity are deeply ingrained in our professional culture. In fact, a 2017 study demonstrated that our culture positively associates busyness with positive traits such as ambition and success – so much so that being busy can be considered a status symbol (Bellezza, Paharia, & Keinan, 2017). However, busyness, stress, and fatigue can have detrimental effects on our cognitive, emotional, and physical well-being. As such, many look for solutions to improve attention, reduce stress, and enhance their ability to focus on the present moment. Mindfulness practices have seen a cultural resurgence as a way to achieve balance amidst our hectic lives.

Practicing mindfulness can encompass a range of activities. Generally, mindfulness has been defined as "the awareness that emerges through paying attention on purpose, in the present moment, and nonjudgmentally to the unfolding of experience moment by moment" (Kabat-Zinn, 2003, p. 144). Individuals can approach this practice in a number of ways, including focusing on their breath, engaging in personal reflection, or following a guided meditation. The concept of mindfulness is more than just a fad or a lifestyle trend. In fact, empirical research supports a variety of positive social and cognitive benefits that result from mindfulness meditation. Most importantly, mindfulness can serve as an effective way to both alter our implicit associations and mitigate the effects of chronic stress (Lueke & Gibson, 2015; Meiklejohn et al., 2012).

> Mindfulness is most often referred to as a "practice" due to the idea that it cannot be mastered completely. Many practice mindfulness daily through guided practices that can be facilitated by technology including apps and audio or visual aids. If you choose to begin a mindfulness practice, you will find a broad selection of books available and apps that can be downloaded to your mobile phone for ease of access.

As discussed earlier, we are more likely to rely on our implicit cognition when we have depleted our cognitive resources. This usually happens under time pressure, when decision-making moments are subjective or based on ambiguous information, or even when we are tired or hungry. It is important to know these constraints are often present – be mindful of these constraints – during important decisions, such as choosing whether to discipline a student or giving feedback to teachers and other staff (Staats, 2014a). Regardless of why our logical decision-making abilities may be compromised, practices such as mindfulness can help us slow down and remain present in the moment rather than relying on seemingly automatic unconscious associations.

Counter-Stereotypical Exemplars

As previously discussed, many of our implicit associations form when we unconsciously internalize stereotypes that exist in our society, regardless of whether we endorse those stereotypes. The concept of using counter-stereotypic exemplars as an intervention to reduce bias reflects the notion that we can counteract negative stereotypes by replacing them with positive impressions. Counter-stereotypic exemplars refer to information, images, or narratives that defy stereotypes or expectations. Many of us already engage in the benefits of counter-stereotypic exemplars as a form of self-empowerment or motivation. For example, we look up to education leaders and activists such as Malala Yousafzai, Booker T. Washington, Gloria Jean Watkins (better known by her pen name, bell hooks), or Hellen Keller for not only defying discrimination based on their identities but also for helping others,who may be less fortunate or marginalized themselves, gain access to education.

Beyond serving as a source of inspiration, reflecting on counter-stereotypic exemplars can actually reduce implicit biases (Blair & Banaji, 1996; Columb & Plant, 2011). In the same way that we form associations by repeated exposure to messages over time, it may be possible to unlearn biases through exposure to new information that uplifts narratives that contrast with typical associations. In practice, this means we can change our existing implicit biases (whether positive or negative) by reinforcing new, different associations.

Like many of the popular topics covered in social psychology research, the scientific evidence on this particular intervention has its fair share of both proponents and skeptics (for support, see Dasgupta & Asgari, 2004; Dasgupta & Greenwald, 2001; Finnegan, Oakhill, & Garnham, 2015; Lai, Hoffman, & Nosek, 2013). For example, some researchers have found the effect of exemplars to be small unless negative exemplars of the majority group were given in tandem with positive exemplars of the minority group (Joy-Gaba & Nosek, 2010). Others have found that the benefits of counter-stereotypes on reducing implicit bias may only exist when one affirms positive associations rather than attempting to negate existing negative stereotypes (Gawronski, Deutsch, Mbirkou, Seibt, & Strack, 2008). Despite these caveats, reflecting on counter-stereotypic exemplars is one of the most simple and practical ways to begin the journey of working against the effects of bias, and it is certainly worth considering as a strategy in your toolkit.

How To Do It

Although it may prove difficult to change implicit associations (Forscher et al., 2018), each of us can incorporate strategies to help prevent our biases from negatively affecting others. When choosing an intervention to implement, there are many variables to consider. For example, some strategies may be more appropriate in a particular setting such as early childhood education. Other strategies may focus on a particular outcome such as interrupting the school-to-prison pipeline (Capatosto, 2015; Quereshi & Okonofua, 2017). To help you along this process, the following practical strategies are offered to help you incorporate decision-making supports, intergroup contact, mindfulness, and counter-stereotypic exemplars in your everyday life and as an educational professional. Figure 5.1 links each strategy to the implicit bias interference strategies we discussed earlier in this chapter.

Join a Committee or Volunteer Group (1)

Many of the same structures that contribute to our implicit biases (e.g., living in segregated communities; working in professions with a high

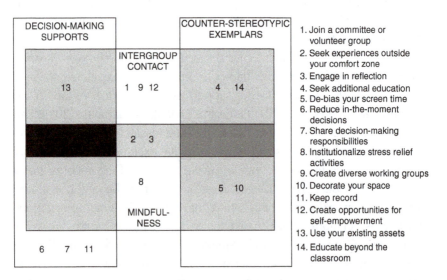

Figure 5.1 Strategies for implicit bias intervention as embedded in the four methods

degree of distractions and time constraints) make it difficult to engage in intergroup contact opportunities as a way to interrupt bias (Dasgupta, 2013; Staats, 2014b). As such, there can be a bit of a "learning curve" as you begin this process and get out of your social comfort zone. Intergroup contact is most effective if it leads to meaningful, ongoing relationships; however, jumping into these interactions can be difficult if you are just beginning your journey. To expose yourself to new opportunities to meet and continually engage with a new group of people with diverse identities, perspectives, and experiences, it can be helpful to join a club or volunteer group. If the purpose of these meetings is to work toward a common goal, such as making your school's community more inclusive or helping facilitate a dialogue to strengthen family-school relationships, then the interaction will be more effective at reducing bias. Modeling our values of equity and inclusion through our behaviors is important in these spaces. We must approach opportunities for intergroup contact without any preconceived expectations. Authenticity and humility are crucial in embracing these interactions as an opportunity to learn – not lead – the conversation.

Seek Experiences Outside Your Comfort Zone (2)

Even if you do not know where to start, a variety of opportunities are readily available to help you listen and learn such as:

- Visiting an international grocery store
- Shopping at establishments owned by people of Color
- Attending an event at a community center on an unfamiliar topic
- Committing to try a guided mindfulness exercise twice a week

Engage in Reflection (3)

Surprisingly, research has demonstrated that even *imagined* contact with people from different backgrounds or identities than yourself is an effective way to minimize the effect of implicit bias (Turner & Crisp, 2010). This is possible because it helps us build empathy and improve our perspective-taking abilities. In a recent review of the literature on imagined intergroup contact, researchers suggested that this technique could be highly beneficial when used in educational settings and offered the following script to help participants engage in imagined contact:

> take a minute to imagine yourself meeting [an outgroup] stranger for the first time. Imagine that the interaction is positive, relaxed and comfortable.
>
> (Crisp, Stathi, Turner, & Husnu, 2009, p. 5)

Take advantage of this strategy by working visualized intergroup contact exercises into your daily routine, whether that is taking some quiet time during your morning commute or by concluding each workday with intentional reflection time.

Seek Additional Education (4)

People with marginalized identities tend to bear the additional burden of educating others about the bias they experience. This dual role of experiencing and educating others about bias can be incredibly taxing. As such, it is important for individuals with "dominant" or "majority" identities to do their own educational work and utilize their privilege to elevate the work of those with marginalized or minoritized identities. To further educate yourself, explore the scholarship and perspectives published by Black, Latinx, and LGBTQ authors. Read narratives that reflect the lived experiences of people with marginalized identities as a way to improve perspective-taking skills. Share these educational resources with your friends and peers and develop space for continued conversations around implicit bias and inequity.

De-Bias Your Screen Time (5)

We are all exposed to a variety of different thoughts, opinions, and ideologies through our technology-driven world. However, as our access to information grows so does the potential for bias in the sources of media we consume. Personalized searches and curated social media may cause us to be exposed only to information that aligns with our existing views. Known as a "filter bubble," this virtual isolation makes it more important than ever to seek additional perspectives and ensure that the media we consume doesn't consistently reaffirm negative stereotypes. Unfortunately, no media outlets are immune to appealing to existing stereotypes, so it is always a helpful practice to ask yourself: Is there a bias in who is consistently being depicted as a victim or perpetrator? Do you see news articles appealing to emotions of fear and hostility rather than sticking to the facts? Consider why media outlets appeal to these stereotypes and themes and for what purpose. These reasons may not always be malicious; in fact, many media outlets appeal to our emotions to spur positive change or social action, but it is still necessary to be mindful of how this information may solidify existing biases.

Reduce In-the-Moment Decisions (6)

In-the-moment decisions are often subject to increased implicit bias – especially when they occur at vulnerable decision points. Whenever possible, buy yourself time and delay judgment until after you have had space and time to reflect on how bias could be a factor. Moreover, try to develop structured time for key decisions. One way to do this is by using a three-step shared decision-making process:

1. Carve out a standard amount of time to address key decisions during staff meetings;
2. Make sure staff have a concrete agenda with clear guidelines to reduce ambiguity; and
3. Bring in outside perspectives as needed.

For example, if you are planning to pilot a new educational program, ensure that a set portion of time during planning meetings is reserved for making decisions (not merely discussion options). If the agenda for one day addresses which students will be served by this program, it would be helpful to outline key questions you want to ask beforehand (e.g., What number of students should be served? What is the ideal student population you want to engage? What will the budget be per pupil?). By making the decisions themselves explicit beforehand, it is easier to prepare for and reflect on the possibility of implicit bias rather than just making decisions as questions surface organically during these meetings.

Share Decision-Making Responsibilities (7)

Incorporate students into school-wide decisions, particularly those that can have a significant impact on school culture or climate. For example, administrators can pilot a formal or informal student discipline council. You can do this by starting at the classroom level and building time into the end of each day (or class period) to discuss and evaluate both positive and negative behaviors. Make sure to get students' input at various stages in this process from planning to implementation. Also, ask students for insight on how to address instances of misbehavior and find ways to incentivize student engagement and prosocial behavior.

Institutionalize Stress-Relief Activities (8)

For many, the idea of practicing mindfulness in a school environment may seem like a distraction from other important activities. However, mindfulness practice contributes to a wide array of benefits. Coincidentally, one of the best ways to combat the long-term effects of implicit bias as adults is also a well-researched intervention for combating chronic stress in youth populations, improving teachers' well-being and self-efficacy, and improving student–teacher interactions (Meiklejohn et al., 2012). Chapter 6 will provide more detail on how to implement mindfulness at the school-wide level.

Create Diverse Working Groups (9)

Schools can provide opportunities to interact with students and staff from different backgrounds that may not be available in their immediate neighborhoods (Telzer, Humphreys, Shapiro, & Tottenham, 2013). Educational leaders may consider the creation of an inclusion working group or task force to meaningfully engage staff and students who are already passionate about these issues. Engaging your staff and student body in a formal working group can reduce the administrative and time burden on any one person to help advance institutional change. When considering the activities and focus of this group, consider the multiplicity of identities your students possess such as race, gender, and LGBTQ identity. Diversity does not occur on a single indicator, but rather it spans several intersectionalities between differences that must all be included.

Fearing the Unknown? When Ingroup Contact Can Really Make a Difference

I was the only person of Color in a large honors classroom with primarily White students. I eventually noticed that every time I bent over to get something from my backpack (paper, pencil, etc.), there would be a sound, and every person on the same row and the row in front of me would grab their backpacks. The first time it happened, I didn't believe my ears and eyes, but I went into my backpack on purpose, and there it was again. I did this about five times just to be sure I was seeing and hearing the same thing. I've thought about how things could have been different in the classroom. Sometimes teachers want groups to choose their own group members. We all know what happens there! What teachers could do is build small communities within large classes, initially assign group roles; teach students the importance of working with others; and have goal building exercises where success is based on the entire team's efforts.

– Donna M. Druery

Decorate Your Space (10)

Whether working in an office, classroom, or school, the décor is often within your control. Try to include images of counter-stereotypes as a way to decorate your school or even just your own personal workspace. Consider how existing images and messages may influence which students may feel welcome and who may not. For example, in their bestselling book *Blindspot: Hidden Biases of Good People*, implicit bias researchers Mahzarin R. Banaji and Anthony G. Greenwald suggested including images of counter-stereotypical exemplars as a computer screensaver as a quick and easy way to integrate an implicit bias intervention into your workday (Banaji & Greenwald, 2013).

Keep Record (11)

It is important to track data to be able to identify where barriers to equity may occur in your classroom or your school. Often the data are the first step in realizing that implicit bias is affecting those around you. Given the immense time pressures and multitasking that takes place in educational settings, it is important to be realistic. You do not need to do a comprehensive data analysis on a daily basis; start small and build up. For example, a good place to start would be working with teachers and other staff to document the impact of key decisions. You can document who gets verbal warnings, classroom-based discipline (e.g., timeouts, moving desks, verbal reprimands), and who gets sent to the office. Track these indicators over a couple weeks and see whether students' identities have any relationship to discipline trends. Alternatively, look at who is doing well in your school, and ask yourself what supports and opportunities helped them succeed. Are these supports and opportunities available to all students? If not, what additional supports can you provide to students who may not have access to supports? Data can even be used to evaluate your curriculum: are all students represented in educational resources? How can you include culturally relevant examples in coursework? These are only a few questions that may be a good place to start your bias-tracking process. Using data in your school is discussed further in the next chapter, and you will find a detailed guide to beginning to use data in your school in Appendix A. Collecting data will set you on the path to tracking important trends over time and may serve as a benchmark for starting a small-scale intervention.

Create Opportunities for Self-Empowerment (12)

Many individuals interested in the pursuit of equity and inclusion are simultaneously marginalized by systems purposed to increase equity and inclusion. Furthermore, the burden of creating an equitable school climate can put many at risk of being scrutinized for their own identities (see Chapter 9 for a personal account). Nevertheless, there is hope. Creating opportunities for self-empowerment is critical for maintaining the sustainability of inclusionary work. Whether this be through self-care, meditation, or building an affinity space for staff who are LGBTQ or of Color, there are many ways to help bring others along on this journey to support and advance empowerment efforts. You are not in this alone.

Use Your Existing Assets (13)

While we will cover more school-wide methods for reducing the negative effects of implicit bias in the next chapter, it is important to consider how you can leverage your personal assets (e.g., your position, relationships, and connections with students) to build the necessary momentum toward institutional change. For example, an immediate task could be to encourage your colleagues to sign a commitment statement to address implicit bias at your school. Work with other colleagues to generate ideas for how to present this information to other school leaders such as administrators, teachers, and mental health staff. While these steps may seem small now, they can ignite the change that will lead to a big impact down the road.

Educate Beyond the Classroom (14)

Even if you do not spend your whole day in the classroom, it is important to think of other non-traditional opportunities to educate both staff and students about implicit bias. Research on the topic of anti-bias pedagogy in K-12 education is very limited; however, evidence from one study demonstrated that college educational seminars on the subjects of prejudice and discrimination reduced students' implicit and explicit anti-Black bias (Rudman, Ashmore, & Gary, 2001). This is why it is so important to take every opportunity to reflect on present and historic ramifications of inequity – both inside and outside the classroom – as a way to work toward collective change in your school. For example, when we approach the topic of racism and discrimination, we often solely focus on the Black–White dichotomy. It may be helpful to integrate educational experiences from other cultures, heritages, and traditions into your school leadership strategy. This could present a great opportunity for students to educate staff and other classmates about their individual backgrounds and identities in ways that are engaging and fun.

Table 5.1 Strategy Shortcut

When...	Consider:
You're tired...	Doing a 5–10 minute guided meditation.
You are unsure of how to make a difference...	How to gather the input of others to help creative innovative ways to address implicit bias.
	Collecting data to see what concerns are most relevant to your staff and student body.
	Looking at district-level data to see what gaps persist.
You're frustrated...	Taking a small break to limit your reliance on bias in moments where you may be most susceptible.
You're making an important decision...	How your implicit biases and current mental state may be unconsciously influencing your decision-making skills.
You want to empower yourself...	Creating formal or informal affinity spaces around your own identities.
You want to engage with your staff and colleagues around issues of implicit bias...	Incorporating implicit bias training or other forms of cultural competence into your professional development strategy or school climate efforts.

Strategy Shortcut

It may be difficult to keep all of these strategies in mind, especially when you are navigating stressful and time-consuming situations in your workplace and personal life. To help support you during these moments, Table 5.1 provides a list of quick strategies to consider: a strategy shortcut. To help you continue to grow on your path to implicit bias remediation, we have provided some blank spaces at the end of the table that you can fill in with your own favorite strategies!

Final Thoughts

While incorporating individual strategies into your implicit bias remediation and reduction practices are a good and necessary step for interrupting the impact of implicit bias, they are not sufficient for creating the long-term change necessary for all students to receive the benefits of our education system. This is why it is so critical to couple our personal efforts and practices with institutional buy-in and a bias-conscious system-based reform effort. Many of the strategies presented in this chapter touched on ways that can impact the broader inequities in the system by explicitly seeking the inclusion of students and staff with marginalized identities into decision-making processes. Interrupting implicit bias in our schools is equally reliant on creating space at the table and ensuring our implicit biases do not invalidate others' perspectives and ideas both during and after the decision-making process. The next chapter will provide strategies of how to interrupt and dismantle the effects of implicit bias in your school.

References

Allport, G. W. (1954). *The nature of prejudice*. Reading, MA: Addison-Wesley.

Banaji, M. R., & Greenwald, A. (2013). *Blindspot: Hidden biases of good people*. New York, NY: Delacorte Press.

Bellezza, S., Paharia, N., & Keinan, A. (2017). Conspicuous consumption of time: When busyness and lack of leisure time become a status symbol. *Journal of Consumer Research, 44*(1), 118–138.

Blair, I. V., & Banaji, M. R. (1996). Automatic and controlled processes in stereotype priming. *Journal of Personality and Social Psychology, 70*(6), 1142–1163.

Brewer, M. B. (1999). The psychology of prejudice: Ingroup love or outgroup hate? *Journal of Social Issues, 55*(3), 429–444.

Capatosto, K. (2015). *Implicit bias strategies: Addressing implicit bias in early childhood education*. Columbus, OH: The Kirwan Institute, Ohio State University. Retrieved from http://kirwaninstitute.osu.edu/wp-content/uploads/2015/06/implicit-bias-strategies.pdf

Columb, C., & Plant, E. A. (2011). Revisiting the Obama effect: Exposure to Obama reduces implicit prejudice. *Journal of Experimental Social Psychology, 47*(2), 499–501.

Crisp, R. J., Stathi, S., Turner, R. N., & Husnu, S. (2009). Imagined intergroup contact: Theory, paradigm, and practice. *Social and*

Personality Psychology Compass, 3(1), 1–18. https://doi.org/10.1111/j.1751-9004.2008.00155.x

Dasgupta, N. (2013). Implicit attitudes and beliefs adapt to situations: A decade of research on the malleability of implicit prejudice, stereotypes, and the self-concept. *Advances in Experimental Social Psychology, 47*(1), 233–279.

Dasgupta, N., & Asgari, S. (2004). Seeing is believing: Exposure to counterstereotypic women leaders and its effect on the malleability of automatic gender stereotyping. *Journal of Experimental Social Psychology, 40*(5), 642–658.

Dasgupta, N., & Greenwald, A.G. (2001). On the malleability of automatic attitudes: Combating automatic prejudice with images of admired and disliked individuals. *Journal of Personality and Social Psychology, 81*(1), 800–814.

Finnegan, E., Oakhill, J., & Garnham, A. (2015). Counter-stereotypical pictures as a strategy for overcoming spontaneous gender stereotypes. *Frontiers in Psychology, 6,* 1291.

Forscher, P. S., Lai, C. K., Axt, J., Ebersole, C. R., Herman, M., Devine, P. G., & Nosek, B. A. (2018, May 21). *A meta-analysis of procedures to change implicit measures.* Retrieved from psyarxiv.com/dv8tu. https://doi.org/10.17605/OSF.IO/DV8TU

Gawronski, B., Deutsch, R., Mbirkou, S., Seibt, B., & Strack, F. (2008). When "just say no" is not enough: Affirmation versus negation training and the reduction of automatic stereotype activation. *Journal of Experimental Social Psychology, 44*(2), 370–377.

Joy-Gaba, J. A., & Nosek, B. A. (2010). The surprisingly limited malleability of implicit racial evaluations. *Social Psychology, 41*(3), 137–146.

Kabat-Zinn, J. (2003). Mindfulness-based intervention in context: Past, present, and future. *Clinical Psychology Science and Practice, 10*(2), 144–156.

Kubota, J. T., Peiso, J., Marcum, K., & Cloutier, J. (2017). Intergroup contact throughout the lifespan modulates implicit racial biases across perceivers' racial group. *PLoS ONE, 12*(7), e0180440. http://doi.org/10.1371/journal.pone.0180440

Lai, C. K., Hoffman, K. M., & Nosek, B. A. (2013). Reducing implicit prejudice. *Social and Personality Psychology Compass, 7,* 315–330.

Lueke, A., & Gibson, B. (2015). Mindfulness meditation reduces implicit age and race bias: The role of reduced automaticity of responding. *Social Psychological and Personality Science, 6*, 284–291.

Meiklejohn, J., Phillips, C., Freedman, M. L., Griffin, M. L., Biegel, G., Roach, A., … Saltzman, A. (2012). Integrating mindfulness training into K-12 education: Fostering the resilience of teachers and students. *Mindfulness, 3*(4), 291–307. www.mindful-well-being.com/wp-content/uploads/2014/07/Meiklejohn-et-al-2012.pdf

Pettigrew, T. F., & Tropp, L. R. (2006). A meta-analytic test of intergroup contact theory. *Journal of Personality and Social Psychology, 90*(5), 751–783.

Pettigrew, T. F., Tropp, L. R., Wagner, U., & Christ, O. (2011). Recent advances in intergroup contact theory. *International Journal of Intercultural Relations, 35*(3), 271–280. https://doi.org/10.1016/j.ijintrel.2011.03.001

Quereshi, A., & Okonofua, J. O. (2017). *Locked out of the classroom: How implicit bias contributes to disparities in school discipline.* New York, NY: NAACP: Legal Defense and Education Fund. Retrieved from www.naacpldf.org/files/about-us/Bias_Reportv2017_30_11_FINAL.pdf

Rudman, L. A., Ashmore, R. D., & Gary, M. L. (2001). "Unlearning" automatic biases: The malleability of implicit prejudice and stereotypes. *Journal of Personality and Social Psychology, 81*(5), 856–868.

Staats, C. (2014a). *Implicit racial bias and school discipline disparities.* Columbus, OH: Kirwan Institute for the Study of Race and Ethnicity. Retrieved from http://kirwaninstitute.osu.edu/wp-content/uploads/2014/05/ki-ib-argument-piece03.pdf

Staats, C. (2014b). *Implicit bias, intergroup contact, and debiasing: Considering neighborhood dynamics.* New York, NY: Furman Center, New York University. Retrieved from, http://furmancenter.org/research/iri/essay/implicit-bias-intergroup-contact-and-debiasing-considering-neighborhood-dyn

Telzer, E. H., Humphreys, K. L., Shapiro, M., & Tottenham, N. (2013). Amygdala sensitivity to race is not present in childhood but emerges over adolescence. *Journal of Cognitive Neuroscience, 25*(2), 234–244. doi:10.1162/jocn_a_00311

Turner, R. N., & Crisp, R. J. (2010). Imagining intergroup contact reduces implicit prejudice. *British Journal of Social Psychology, 49*, 129–142.

Van Ryn, M., & Saha, S. (2011). Exploring unconscious bias in disparities research and medical education. *Journal of the American Medical Association, 306*(9), 995–996.

Vezzali, L., & Giovannini, D. (2011). Intergroup contact and reduction of explicit and implicit prejudice toward immigrants: A study with Italian businessmen owning small and medium enterprise. *Quality & Quantity, 45*(1), 213–222.

Making a Difference in Your School
Institutional Strategies

Introduction

Now that you are prepared to make some changes in the way you approach situations involving the possibility of implicit bias, you can begin to reflect on how you can catalyze school-wide change as a school leader. Many of the same strategies you learned to change your own behavior can be implemented at the school-wide level with the help of focused and targeted professional development, but these will not work in isolation. Sustainable school changes require cultural and climate changes that permeate the entire school community. At the core of any successful school-wide change is a high-quality leader, which means you may need to focus on your individual skills before trying to implement lasting change for implicit bias remediation and reduction. Even when the impact of changes is great, it is important you remain mindful of the integrity and intent of the changes made – remember that as a leader you must lead the change and be the change in synchrony; only then will your efforts hold the potential for lasting and meaningful impact.

Extensions of Self Strategies

In the last chapter we focused on decision-making supports, intergroup contact, mindfulness, and counter-stereotypic exemplars. All four of these can be facilitated in a top-down approach to school management. While the obvious answer would seem to be to provide professional development to teachers and staff on these techniques, you also can ingrain these practices into school and district norms through policy and practice.

Decision-Making Supports

Decision-making is at the heart of implicit (and explicit) bias in schools, so it's not surprising that supports are so effective. Organizations have long explored how to use shared and structured decision-making to heighten workplace and economic efficacy (Katz & Kahn, 1966, 1980; Duncan, 1973). As implied in the names, shared decision-making is when multiple people contribute to a decision, and structured is when there is a set form for making decisions. Last chapter we talked about sharing decision-making responsibilities such as through a student discipline council. Restorative Practices, which we will discuss further later in this chapter, offers the restorative conference as one way in which students and educators can share discipline-related decision responsibilities. Here, a student offender, student victim, and school professional have a conference to focus on how to make reparations to the victim in response to a targeted disciplinary infraction – the three participants *share* the decision. Shared decision-making can also occur at higher levels such as principal–teacher or superintendent–principal. In these higher-level shared processes, decisions tend to focus more on policy and practices. Many schools form teams or committees to develop or update school codes of conduct or to choose curriculum. These are examples of shared decision-making. While it seems natural and democratic for many to choose school- or district-wide impactors this way, it is also a way to avoid bias by keeping the opinions diverse and in check. Schools can go a step further to diversify the people involved in the shared decision-making process, including traditionally underserved populations (racial minority, low-income, special needs) as well as key stakeholders (students, teachers, community representatives, social justice group representatives, etc.). Just as shared decision-making creates a more equity-focused and generally more acceptable decision-making process, structured decision-making provides a stream-lined and consistent approach to decisions.

School leaders implementing structured decision-making can develop decision flow charts (see Quinlan, 1990), adopt decision-making plans, or provide professional development in decision thought processes (Gregory

& Failing, 2012). Flow charts, or decision trees, are commonly seen in discipline plans and codes of conduct and help school professionals to determine an outcome in response to a specific infraction. Another application of flow charts is to help guide the process for student identification for special education services like that seen in Figure 6.1.

While charts like these offer a way to help remove implicit bias from decisions by standardizing the processes, they come with limitations as

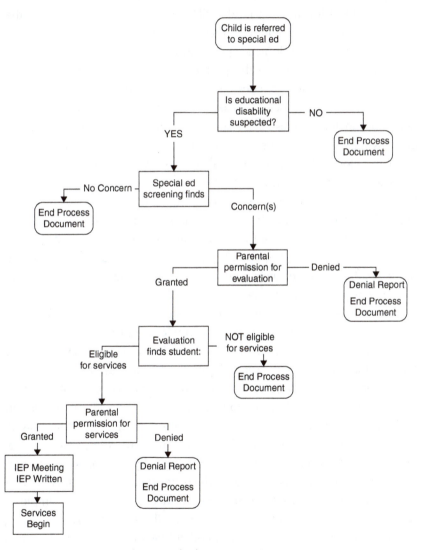

Figure 6.1 Decision tree for special education services

well. Such rigid decision trees are difficult to apply when answers are vague. Let's say that only one of two parents sharing custody grants permission in the decision tree in Figure 6.1. In this case the process is muddied; as such, schools should provide information on what to do when situations do not fit the mold if structured decision-making is implemented in this way.

Decision-making processes and thought processes focus more on the steps involved when making a decision rather than the specific decisions. One popular version of structured decision-making, simply called the Structured Decision Making model (SDM model), is borrowed from the environmental sciences and most recently popularized by Robin Gregory and Lee Failing (2012). In its simplest form, this model breaks a problem into seven steps: (1) define the problem, (2) determine the objectives, (3) identify alternatives, (4) consider potential consequences, (5) consider tradeoffs and risk tolerance, (6) make the decision, and (7) monitor linked decisions. In these steps, individuals or teams go through the process of knowing what they are setting out to fix and why they aim to fix that problem before delving into potential choices; once all choices are identified and considered by impact, decisions are made and monitored to offer learning and highlight new problems should they emerge. Yusuf, Irvine, and Bell (2016) worked with a school where shared decision-making was used to develop a structured decision-making tool unique to the school where it was created. They found that through this process and the use of the resulting tool, teachers were more aware of biases and focused on reducing disparities in their decisions as well.

Other systems offer embedded shared *and* structural decision-making as well. Positive Behavior Interventions and Supports (see Sugai & Horner, 2006) and in particular Culturally Responsive Positive Behavior Interventions and Supports (see Bal, 2018) offer structure to the decision-making process by setting up a system of observation and levels of response. Even the Response to Interventions framework for special needs support and identification provides a starting point for teachers to know how to respond to students in various situations of need (Bradley, Danielson, & Doolittle, 2005). Each of these approaches typically has embedded systems of accountability and data usage, which we detail later in this chapter and further in Appendix A. Even a plan for decision-making as simple as delaying potentially emotional decisions until the school day following an incident provides the space for implicit bias to be acknowledged and avoided (remember emotion influences decisions: see Loewenstein &

Lerner, 2003). No matter the chosen approach, supported decisions are better decisions – especially when considering implicit bias in schools.

Intergroup Contact

Making intergroup contact on your own is not only a great way to reduce implicit bias (Gaertner & Dovidio, 2014), but it also is a great networking tool that can lead to reduced bias-related incidents in your school. As a leader, you lead by example and offer direction to others in the school. Intergroup contact by a leader might be as simple as stepping into the community served by the school or simply creating opportunities where you can spend time with students. To bring intergroup contact into your school you can begin by focusing on two areas: (1) recruiting and retaining a diverse faculty and (2) community integration and involvement.

Recruiting and Retaining a Diverse Faculty

While possibly the most challenging of the three, recruitment and reten-tion of a diverse faculty is most likely to provide intergroup contact to the greatest number of individuals. School professionals interact frequently due to the need for collaborative work in planning, professional development, and day-to-day school operations. Hiring a diverse staff (besides teachers) is, of course, similarly helpful; however, making sure to diversify faculty in addition to staff is important to counteract the common implicit associ-ation of the White female teacher. In hiring teachers of different races and ethnicities, different genders, different abilities, and so forth, you create a counter-narrative to that traditional image. Furthermore, students have better outcomes in schools where more teachers are culturally or racially matched with the population – especially students of Color (Dee, 2004).

Focused recruitment for diversity comes with many caveats that focus both on the current staff's feelings of infiltration and new staff's support and inclusion in the workplace climate. Leaders must get staff on board with targeted recruitment and plan for retention. McKay and Avery (2005) address this in their paper: "Warning! Diversity Recruitment Could Backfire!"

While the thought of a diverse workforce is quite simple, many struggle with the execution. Leaders can post jobs to diverse job networks such as the National Alliance of Black School Educators (NABSE), Latinos for Education, and LGBT Connect; network with Historically Black Colleges and Universities (HBCUs) with teacher certification programs; create positive and inclusive workplaces for educators of Color or gender minority; and reach out to families in diverse school districts with children interested in pursuing careers in education. To retain teachers once hired, schools should support new teachers as they find affinity groups and avoid a "token" culture where one non-majority teacher is taken as the voice for his or her entire population. While some teachers might be amenable to providing some insights related to cultural differences, no one person can speak for an entire group of people or should ever be expected to do so. In addition, leaders should pair new teachers with experienced mentors – especially when beginning to introduce diversity into a school's faculty. Current faculty must feel involved rather than imposed in order for the new faculty to be in a safe and positive career path. Leaders must take initiative and responsibility to create a school culture where that is possible.

Community Integration and Involvement

Community integration and involvement is a slightly easier method of intergroup contact, but it may incite pushback from staff due to the increased expectations associated with the practice. Principals can create an inclusive culture that welcomes parents into the school by providing opportunities for parents to visit or volunteer at the school. When possible, areas of the school can be used for community events such as yard sales, dinners, or holiday celebrations. Teachers can be asked to visit community events (and you should also attend if possible) such as church breakfasts, sporting events, festivals, recitals, and health fairs. When school professionals contribute regularly to the community, the increased collaboration and engagement between the school and community establishes opportunities for intergroup contact. Leaders must, however, be respectful of the additional expectations this kind of culture places on teachers and staff; consider how participants will be compensated (perhaps non-monetarily) for efforts, and recognize that you will need to lead by example.

Mindful Practices for Decision-Making

While mindfulness was discussed in the previous chapter as it relates more to grounded awareness often embedded in meditation, mindfulness at the school-wide level is more often focused on explicit awareness and communication. Awareness of implicit bias may be established by measuring individual biases using the tools described in Chapter 2 (Implicit Association Test, Affective Priming Task, Affect Misattribution Procedure) and built upon by discussing reactions and meaning through communicative professional development sessions. For example, after school-admittance decision-makers measured their own implicit biases at one medical school, the following year of accepted students was by far the most diverse the school had ever enrolled (Capers, Clinchot, McDougle, & Greenwald, 2017). While this study did not include an introduction to the measurement tool or follow-up discussion of results, implicit bias awareness was linked with a positive change toward increased student diversity. In Chapter 8, you will see how thoughtfully embedding implicit bias measurement can help to contextualize and clarify this awareness – in turn creating a culture where mindful reflection becomes the norm.

Other methods of increasing conscious awareness are found in delayed decision-making, the "write it out" approach to discipline, and Restorative Practices' circles. As discussed earlier, delaying decisions – particularly discipline decisions – allows for reduced emotionality and lowers the cognitive load during the decision, which in turn decreases the influence of implicit biases (Loewenstein & Lerner, 2003). The pause also gives time for thought and mindful decision-making. In the "write it out" method of discipline, a decision-maker must write out what happened in the class and why an office disciplinary referral is most appropriate prior to making any such referrals. Following a "write it out" referral, the decider of the disciplinary outcome also writes out why the particular outcome was chosen (this can also work to provide extra documentation in the event of a legal or special education follow up). Many schools using this method also choose to have the students write out what they did, why they were referred, and what they think would be an appropriate response. This helps to act as a learning tool and may also create stronger relationships and understanding between students and school professionals similar to that seen in Restorative Practices' circles (Mansfield, Fowler, & Rainbolt, 2018). In these circles, a victim of an incident sits with a moderator and the perpetrator to discuss what happened and what would be an appropriate method for restoring peace. Here, with effective communication several individuals can work together mindfully toward a solution.

Sometimes communicating about sensitive topics, such as race or gender, presents an additional challenge to overcoming implicit biases. Staff should have an agreed-upon vocabulary for talking about differences and be encouraged to develop this vocabulary in an accepting and educational setting. Many programs offer structure for effective discussion such as Fierce Conversations (Scott, 2004) and Courageous Conversations (Singleton, 2014; Singleton & Linton, 2005). Some basic underpinnings of these communication approaches involve:

- Using "I" statements (When you did that I felt...; In my experiences I usually see; I did...)
- Focusing on positive statements
- Understanding individuals share lived experiences only
- Avoiding shame and judgement
- Making statements without qualifiers such as "but"
- Sitting with and accepting discomfort.

Formal practice of mindfulness meditation in schools is quite valuable (Meiklejohn et al., 2012). Mindfulness can be direct where students are explicitly taught to use mindfulness, indirect where teachers practice and model mindfulness, or combined perhaps with students learning how to use mindfulness from teachers' targeted modeling as instruction. Some mindfulness programs are designed specifically for the use of teachers such as Mindfulness-Based Wellness Education (MBWE; see Poulin, Mackenzie, Soloway, & Karayolas, 2008), Cultivating Awareness and Resilience in Education (CARE), and Stress Management and Relaxation Techniques (SMART; see Jennings, Lantieri, & Roeser, 2011). All of these programs focus on the use of mindfulness as it relates to socio-emotional well-being and can act through increased awareness during decision-making processes.

Not formally a mindfulness strategy but well within the spirit, Situational Attribution Training has users consider the situation of a student rather than the student's disposition when making decisions – most often disciplinary decisions (Stewart, Latu, Kawakami, & Myers, 2010). In this manner, teachers less often rely on assumed, automatic stereotypes for information when making decisions due to a practiced reliance on more contextual aspects of the situation. Together, mindfulness-based approaches to implicit bias reduction offer systemic and low-cost tools for effective change.

Counter-Stereotypic Exemplars

At the school-wide level, counter-stereotypic exemplars work by exposing individuals to astereotypical examples of stereotyped individuals. While principals cannot force such exposure, counter-examples may be embedded into school policy and practice through (1) books for faculty summer reading or those used in the curriculum, (2) curriculum focus on counter-stereotypical historical figures, (3) invited speakers and assembly choices, (4) screen savers and posters, (5) targeted field trips, and (6) diversity in invited and recognized heroes. Look for opportunities to introduce your staff and faculty to community leaders that are representative of the student population and to free resources on the web such as the Implicit Bias Initiative of the American Bar Association. Moreover, be mindful of the resources, activities, and décor presented in the school to ensure that all kinds of students are represented and that representations do not perpetuate stereotypical conceptualizations. While individuals must accept counter-stereotypes on their own terms, school leaders can facilitate opportunities for growth.

Countering the Stereotypes in the Classroom

Dirty Little Prisons: Stopping the Pipeline One Couch and Plant at a Time
As I walked into the Baltimore County Department of Corrections, I heard the door slam shut behind me. I was ushered into a room with lockers and ordered to put my belongings in *my* designated locker, so I did. As I walked down the dimly lit hallway, I felt angst. Armed guards with metal detecting wands waving them against my brown arms and

legs. Bells chiming – indicting when it was time for the inmates to transition. The windows were cloudy and stained – making it impossible to see out of them – all of this to visit my oldest brother: a high school dropout who had, in my estimation, been funneled through an educational system and filtered right into the prison system.

Days later, I walked into another Baltimorean edifice. I experienced the same hard slam of the door behind me; the same ushering of individuals to lockers; and the same dimly illuminated hallways. Guards with metal detectors and weapons, chiming bells – moving bodies from one transition to the next. I saw the same cloudy, stained windows; however, this time, I was in the school where I taught.

I never before reflected on the perils and parallels of schools and prisons even though it was right in front of me. This form of observational selection bias reaffirmed that I wasn't making extraordinary connections as if these similarities were new, but rather I'd finally opened my eyes to see how implicit *I* was in the perpetuation of it all. Days later, plugin air fresheners, plants, reading couches, lights, and more all found their way into my classroom. I was determined to revive my surroundings to make school feel, look, and smell more like school and less like a prison – for my students and for me.

– Brandon Wallace

School-Wide Strategies

While many individual strategies are effective when applied as a school-wide approach, the systemic nature of schools makes several other interventions appropriate for reducing and remediating the effects of implicit bias. Some of the methods we will discuss in this section include accountability, discipline systems, professional development interventions, policy changes, and relationship building. Even so, there is one element that is critical to school-wide implicit bias remediation and change in general: data. Most strategies rely heavily on knowing whether there is a problem and understanding what that problem entails. If you don't know if there are inequities between your students and where those inequities exist, you cannot know if your strategy use is effective or even necessary (Carter, Skiba, Arredondo, & Pollock, 2014).

The remainder of this chapter will begin with a discussion of data use through equity audits, equity traps, and school climate assessments. Using data in schools is further detailed in Appendix A. The chapter then proceeds to describe more specific school-wide strategies for the remediation of implicit bias in schools (with some relation to how it looks in the data).

Data-Based Strategies

Equity Audits

A systemic approach to using data for school equity, equity audits, are attributed to Skrla, Scheurich, Garcia, and Nolly (2004) and described in detail in the 2009 book by Skrla, McKenzie, and Scheurich. The equity audit involves three dimensions: (1) teacher quality equity, (2) programmatic equity, and (3) achievement equity, where the first two sum to the third.

Teacher Quality + Programmatic Equity = Achievement Equity

Table 6.1 breaks down these domains into observable variables, which are then analyzed. Skrla and colleagues suggested a multi-step analysis process similar to the data cycle described in Appendix A for equity audits that begins with gathering a committee of stakeholders to perform the audits who are then presented with some of the data collected. The next step has the committee discuss gaps and meet with experts to better understand the problem in order to form a plan. The plan is implemented and monitored for results, which are then celebrated if successful or revisited with a new solution if unsuccessful. When linked with implicit bias remediation goals, the committee looks for differences before and after general school-wide trainings or interventions. If some improvements are deemed unsatisfactory, more specifically targeted improvements may be added for those involved, such as use of the "write it out" method in decision-making or opportunities for use of more individual strategies as discussed in Chapter 5. This data structure offers one of many approaches to data use in schools for monitoring implicit bias-related goals. For a more detailed discussion of how to use data in schools, see Appendix A.

Table 6.1 Observable Variables by Equity Audit Domain and Related Criteria

Domain	Criteria	Variables
Teacher Quality	Teacher Education	# or % by degree type
	Teacher Experience	# of years as a teacher
	Teacher Mobility	# or % leaving annually
	Teacher Certification	# or % uncertified
		# or % teaching outside certification area
Programmatic	Special Education	Discrepancy: % enrolled overall compared to % enrolled in each subgroup
	Gifted & Talented	Discrepancy in enrollment
	Bilingual Education	% bilingual students proficient in reading
	Student Discipline	Discrepancy in exclusionary discipline
Achievement	State Test Scores	State standardized test scores
	Dropout Rates	Dropout or HS completion rate
	HS Graduation Tracks	% of graduates in each track
	SAT/ACT/AP	Scores

Equity Traps

While a formal process of data is helpful, it does not answer all the questions. McKenzie and Scheurich (2004) discuss using what they term "equity traps" to attend to vulnerable decision points (remember that vulnerable decision points are more subject to the effects of implicit bias). The equity trap approach has teachers and staff write in journals and participate in interviews that ask one question: Why don't your X students perform comparably to your Y students? This qualitative data is used to discover the presence of any of the four equity traps in school practices: (1) deficit thinking, (2) racial erasure, (3) avoided or employed gaze, and (4) paralogical beliefs and actions. Deficit thinking is a focus on what students or a stereotyped group cannot do rather than what they can, while racial erasure refers to pretending that students have no differences at all akin to colorblindness. Avoided gaze is when teachers avoid attending to students of a certain group while employed gaze is an over-attention (like looking at Black boys more often for problem behaviors in Gilliam and colleague's 2016 article). Paralogical beliefs and actions refer to when someone illogically attributes something to a person based on stereotypes or expectations. Each of the four types of equity traps offer a different form of bias that may occur as an implicit bias: assuming students cannot do something because they have less income; assuming all students have the same background knowledge; looking at the Asian student to answer questions more often; asking the Mexican student to bring in tacos – all without realizing the bias-driven assumptions. These "traps" are common areas where interventions at the school level can occur that often are invisible when using numeric, or quantitative, data alone.

School Climate

Ross (2013) wrote, "Equity is intrinsic to all aspects of school climate work" (p. 1) and went on to discuss how high expectations, healthy learning environments, caring relationships, and meaningful participation and engagement support such equity. As such, many schools use climate measures to evaluate school equity and drive interventions. One measure of this nature is the School Climate Measure (Zullig, Koopman, Patton, & Ubbes, 2010; Zullig et al. 2015). This measure has students rate a series of statements on an agree/disagree scale to numerically assess climate. While this measure is good for many, other districts create measures unique to their school and specific needs. Climate data should include the input of parents, students, teachers, and administrators whenever possible to account for all involved perspectives. In the simplest form, informal discussion with stakeholders is a way to learn more about climate. While the connection to implicit bias through school climate is less explicit, the climate reflects the presence of a culture that either accepts or rejects biased actions. When a school achieves a positive climate where all students are accepted, bias (implicit and explicit) is socially unacceptable. Together these various forms of data collection and use provide mechanisms to drive changes toward remediating the effects of implicit bias in schools.

Accountability

Very much linked to data is the use of accountability systems in schools. While teacher accountability has been widely normalized as part of and following the No Child Left Behind era, school accountability has been limited to student academic growth in the public eye. As a school leader, you are more acutely aware of the vastness of accountability inclusive of discipline, safety, teacher turnover, finances, and other indicators of school performance. As you might expect, when school professionals are held accountable for decisions, they are more likely to consciously attend to those decisions, in turn increasing decision accuracy (Cate, Krolak-Schwerdt, & Glock, 2016). In their 2016 study, Cate and her team gave teachers vignettes about students of various races and asked them to place the students in different academic tracks. When teachers were reminded that they would be held accountable for decisions just prior to making the choices, differences in tracking decisions based on student races (authors called this implicit bias) disappeared. It seems that rather than the actual act of accountability, the reminder that teachers were responsible for their decisions was powerful enough to overcome racial implicit biases.

Discipline Systems

Culturally Responsive Positive Behavior Interventions and Supports

School-Wide Positive Behavior Interventions and Supports (SW-PBIS) is – in short – a three-tiered approach to behavior management at the school-wide level including universal supports for all students, group-level supports for some students, and individual supports for a small number of students (Sugai et al., 2000). While this system is quite successful at lowering the overall levels of exclusionary discipline, it has not been shown to reliably lessen the gap between Black and White students (Vincent & Tobin, 2010). One possible reason for this and similar patterns seen when using academic tiered systems like Response-to-Intervention may be a lack of modification for cultural or contextual appropriateness (Sugai & Horner, 2006). Vincent and colleagues (2010) suggested that schools incorporate components of cultural responsiveness in SW-PBIS by (1) enhancing the self- and cultural-awareness and knowledge of staff, (2) committing to the support of students' cultural practices, and (3) practicing culturally valid decision-making practices. In essence, many of these suggestions align to previously discussed implicit bias remediation strategies such as mindfulness and shared/structured decision-making that are embedded into systems of SW-PBIS. Unfortunately, the three components mentioned above provide only vague strategies, and so Culturally Responsive SW-PBIS (CR-PBIS) was formalized as a five-process practice by Bal and colleagues (2016), as outlined in Table 6.2.

Table 6.2 Culturally Responsive SW-PBIS Process with Embedded Implicit Bias Remediation Strategies

Step in Process	Details/Comments	Embedded Implicit Bias Remediation Strategies
1. Form CR-PBIS learning labs (see Bal, Schrader, Afacan, & Mawene, 2016)	Learning Lab: "a research and innovation site for organic, equity-oriented systemic transformation… Activities focus on developing and facilitating social agency" (Bal, 2018, p. 12). Put together groups of stakeholders that can critically reflect and develop solutions. Groups should include school practitioners, members of the local community, students with their caretakers, skilled behavior interventionists, teachers, and school leaders. Together, learning labs will work to develop home-grown equity plans that give voice and agency to the cultural communities involved.	Shared Decision-Making Intergroup Contact
2. Determine desired outcomes of CR-PBIS	"Make sure to establish a process in which all stakeholders have power over the determination of outcomes – not just voice their concerns" (Bal, 2018, p. 16).	Structured Decision-Making Shared Decision-Making Mindfulness
3. Understand/ use empirically validated practices that are culturally relevant	Use tools such as special education teams, Google Scholar searches, local universities, and advocacy groups to learn about evidenced approaches. Make sure your plan is "democratic, reciprocal, and inclusive [of] school climate, communities of learners, and conceptions of knowledge and curriculum content" (Bal, 2018, p. 19).	Mindfulness Data-Based Decision-Making Intergroup Contact Cultural Relevance

(*continued*)

Table 6.2 (Cont.)

Step in Process	Details/Comments	Embedded Implicit Bias Remediation Strategies
4. Use data-based decision-making	See Appendix A	Data-Based Decision-Making
5. Create systemic change	Build social agency and capacity through the use of coalitions that can work collaboratively with community members and as social and democratic activists.	Intergroup Contact Shared Decision-Making

As the table shows, the CR-PBIS approach embodies many of the systemic strategies shown to help remediate the effects of implicit bias in schools. The system provides a more structured plan for discipline without implicit bias inclusive of a structured implementation plan. CR-PBIS is not simple, but as a combination of different theoretical approaches to discipline disparities shown to work in urban and diverse school settings, it can help schools begin the implicit bias remediation process (See Bal [2018] for more information on how to implement this approach in your school or visit www.CRPBIS.org.)

Restorative Practices/Justice

Restorative Practices has gained popularity as an educational equity tool for discipline in the last decade from international sources (Blood & Thorsborne, 2005; McCluskey et al., 2008) and in more recent years, American sources (Gregory, Clawson, Davis, & Gerewitz, 2016; Mansfield et al., 2018). Restorative conferences/circles are a common element of restorative practices that particularly align with implicit bias remediation strategies. In this practice, victims, offenders, and their communities of care discuss incidents and decide (via shared decision-making) on reparations using "fair processes" and other tools in Restorative Practices such as "the nine affects" and "shame compass." Many other practices embody previously discussed strategies for implicit bias remediation, which Gregory and her team (2016) placed in either preventative (before incidents) domains or in intervention (after incidents) domains. When implemented with high fidelity, Restorative Practices are capable of nearly ameliorating discipline gaps by race in urban settings (Mansfield et al., 2018); however, improper implementation has been linked to maintained racial divides (Lustick, 2015). As such, this discipline system – like most others – offers only a systemic tool usages plan for gap reduction rather than a standalone method for removing the effects of implicit bias in schools. Discipline systems provide effective structure for schools focused on gap reduction, but attitudinal and behavior changes that dissuade implicitly biased decisions must be embedded for meaningful gains.

Professional Development Interventions

Implicit bias trainings have gained popularity in recent years, with numerous companies and consultants offering sessions aimed at raising awareness and addressing the effects of implicit bias. While many of these programs are high quality, some intervention programs have empirical validation as well. While you will read about structuring your own evidence-based system in Chapter 8, another such program was developed by Devine, Forscher, Austin, and Cox (2012). This intervention treats implicit bias as a habit that can be broken through awareness, concern about the effects of bias, and strategy application. The intervention encompasses two stages. First, participants take the Implicit Association Test followed by a training on what their scores mean and how implicit bias might affect their behavior. The second stage trains participants on five strategies to decrease implicit bias:

1. Stereotype replacement: acknowledging stereotypic responses and consciously changing them
2. Counter-stereotypic imaging
3. Individualizing: focusing on personal rather than stereotypic attributes of others
4. Perspective-taking
5. Intergroup contact.

To validate the intervention, an Implicit Association Test was retaken by both participants and non-participants; intervention participants showed drastic reductions in implicit bias that were greater if they had concerns about discrimination and a personal awareness of bias at any point during the study. This study showed that the intervention was effective and implicit bias could be reduced.

Policy Reformation

Like many school-wide issues, policy can serve to change practices through the addition of guidelines for practice, laws, and regulations. In Chapter 7 you will see how an Illinois group responded to policy changes that enforced a need for implicit bias remediation. Other laws focused on discrepancies include the Every Student Succeeds Act (ESSA), which requires schools to report either gaps or progress toward narrowing gaps for both academics and discipline through disaggregated data by race and IEP eligibility. Superintendents and school board members might consider if implicit bias remediation or related accountability is relevant and effective in their own districts. Remember to plan for enforcement and data-based monitoring to make policies more effective.

Relationships

Relationships are definitely not last on the list of effective school-wide strategies for implicit bias remediation, but rather we've saved the best for last. While it's not acceptable to say that you cannot be racist because you have one "X" friend, it is acceptable to recognize that you are likely not acting on implicit "X" biases when with that friend. This is the core of overcoming implicit bias. When you develop a relationship with someone, you need not rely on stereotypes or assumptions because you have genuine information. In a qualitative study of school principals and their impressions of "doing discipline," Kennedy and colleagues (2017) heard one word quite often with respect to principals' disciplinary practices: relationships. In fact, in an ongoing 2018 study trying to better understand how principals make discipline decisions in general, Gullo is hearing much the same. Principals seem to make decisions about students that reflect relationships and work toward building relationships with students, faculty, staff, and community whenever possible.

Not only are relationships important in counteracting implicit bias, but they have the potential to narrow discipline and achievement gaps as well. Positive relationships appear more beneficial to the future success of students from traditionally underserved backgrounds (den Brok, van Tartwijk, Wubbels, & Veldman, 2010), and positive teacher–student relationships are linked to both increased student engagement and higher achievement (Roorda, Koomen, Spilt, & Oort, 2011). If we can build positive relationships with students, that is a significant step toward countering unwanted implicit biases and creating a more welcoming place for students in schools.

Moving Forward

As a leader, you are now tasked with a large job of great importance: working against the effects of implicit bias in your school. We have provided you with tools and strategies to begin this process, but now the onus is on you. In the last part of this book we will provide you with some case examples of people in the field who are doing the work in implicit bias. The first case introduces work to build on policy changes, the second on development of an intervention system, and the third on a school leader's experiences during this change process. The chapters will discuss the journey and lessons learned to best equip you to do this work in your own district or school.

References

American Bar Association. (2018). ABA: Implicit bias initiative. Retrieved from www.americanbar.org/groups/litigation/initiatives/task-force-implicit-bias.html

Bal, A. (2015). *Culturally responsive positive behavioral interventions and supports* (Working Paper No. 2015–9). Wisconsin Center for Education Research: University of Wisconsin-Madison. Retrieved from www.wcer.wisc.edu/publications/workingPapers/papers.php

Bal, A. (2018). Culturally responsive positive behavioral interventions and supports: A process–oriented framework for systemic transformation. *Review of Education, Pedagogy, and Cultural Studies, 40*(2), 144–174. https://doi.org/10.1080/10714413.2017.1417579

Bal, A., Schrader, E. M., Afacan, K., & Mawene, D. (2016). Using learning labs for culturally responsive positive behavioral interventions and supports. *Intervention in School and Clinic, 52*(2), 122–128. https://doi.org/10.1177/1053451216636057

Blood, P., & Thorsborne, M. (2005, March). The challenge of culture change: Embedding restorative practice in schools. In *6th International Conference on Conferencing, Circles and other Restorative Practices,'Building a Global Alliance for Restorative Practices and Family Empowerment* (pp. 3–5). Sydney, Australia.

Bradley, R., Danielson, L, & Doolittle, J. (2005). Response to intervention. *Journal of Learning Disabilities, 38*(6), 485–486. https://doi.org/10.1177/00222194050380060201

Capers, Q. I., Clinchot, D., McDougle, L., & Greenwald, A. G. (2017). Implicit racial bias in medical school admissions. *Academic Medicine, 92*(3), 365–369.

Carter, P., Skiba, R. J., Arredondo, M., & Pollock, M. (2014). *You can't fix what you don't' look at: Acknowledging race in addressing racial discipline disparities. Discipline Disparities: A Research-to-Practice Collaborative.* Retrieved from http://youthjusticenc.org/download/education-justice/disparities/Acknowledging-Race_121514-2.pdf

Cate, I. M. P., Krolak-Schwerdt, S., & Glock, S. (2016). Accuracy of teachers' tracking decisions: Short- and long-term effects of accountability. *European Journal of Psychology of Education, 31*(2), 225–243.

Dee, T. S. (2004). Teachers, race, and student achievement in a randomized experiment. *The Review of Economics and Statistics, 86*(1), 195–210.

den Brok, P., van Tartwijk, J., Wubbels, T., & Veldman, I. (2010). The differential effect of the teacher–student interpersonal relationship on student outcomes for students with different ethnic backgrounds. *British Journal of Educational Psychology, 80*(2), 199–221. https://doi.org/10.1348/000709909X465632

Devine, P. G., Forscher, P. S., Austin, A. J., & Cox, W. T. (2012). Long-term reduction in implicit race bias: A prejudice habit-breaking intervention. *Journal of Experimental Social Psychology, 48*(6), 1267–1278.

Duncan, R. B. (1973). Multiple decision-making structures in adapting to environmental uncertainty: The impact on organizational effectiveness. *Human Relations, 26*(3), 273–291.

Gaertner, S. L., & Dovidio, J. F. (2014). *Reducing intergroup bias: The common ingroup identity model*. London, UK: Psychology Press.

Gilliam, W. S., Maupin, A. N., Reyes, C. R., Accavitti, M., & Shic, F. (2016). *Do early educators' implicit biases regarding sex and race relate to behavior expectations and recommendations of preschool expulsions and suspensions?* Yale University Child Study Center. Retrieved from https://medicine.yale.edu/childstudy/zigler/publications/Preschool%20 Implicit%20Bias%20Policy%20Brief_final_9_26_276766_5379_ v1.pdf

Gregory, A., Clawson, K., Davis, A., & Gerewitz, J. (2016). The promise of Restorative Practices to transform teacher-student relationships and achieve equity in school discipline. *Journal of Educational and Psychological Consultation, 26*(4), 325–353. https://doi.org/10.1080/ 10474412.2014.929950

Gregory, R., & Failing, L. (Eds.). (2012). *Structured decision making: A practical guide to environmental management choices*. Edison, NJ: John Wiley & Sons.

Gullo, G. (2018, June 25). Principals' and discipline decisions: From the voice on the loudspeaker. Retrieved from www.researchgate. net/project/Implicit-Bias-in-School-Disciplinary-Decisions/update/ 5b3136c7b53d2f8928978a03

Jennings, P., Lantieri, L., & Roeser, R. W. (2011). Supporting educational goals through cultivating mindfulness. In A. Higgins-D'Alessandro, M. Corrigan, & P. M. Brown (Eds.), *The handbook of prosocial education* (pp. 371–397). Lanham, MD: Rowman & Littlefield.

Katz, D., & Kahn, R. L. (1966). *The social psychology of organizations*. New York, NY: Wiley.

Katz, D., & Kahn, R. L. (1980). *The social psychology of organizations*. New York, NY: Wiley.

Kennedy, B. L., Murphy, A. S., & Jordan, A. (2017). Title I middle school administrators' beliefs and choices about using corporal punishment and exclusionary discipline. *American Journal of Education, 123*(2), 243–280.

Loewenstein, G., & Lerner, J. S. (2003). The role of affect in decision making. In R. Davidson, H. Goldsmith, & K. Scherer (Eds.), *Handbook of affective science* (pp. 619–642). Oxford: Oxford University Press.

Lustick, H. (2015). Administering discipline differently: A Foucauldian lens on restorative school discipline. *International Journal of Leadership in Education, 20*(3), 1–15.

Mansfield, K. C., Fowler, B., & Rainbolt, S. (2018). The potential of Restorative Practices to ameliorate discipline gaps: The story of one high school's leadership team. *Educational Administration Quarterly, 54*(2), 303–323. https://doi.org/10.1177/0013161X17751178

McCluskey, G., Lloyd, G., Kane, J., Riddell, S., Stead, J., & Weedon, E. (2008). Can restorative practices in schools make a difference? *Educational Review, 60*(4), 405–417. https://doi.org/10.1080/00131910802393456

McKay, P. F., & Avery, D. R. (2005). Warning! Diversity recruitment could backfire. *Journal of Management Inquiry, 14*(4), 330–336.

McKenzie, K. B., & Scheurich, J. J. (2004). Equity traps: A useful construct for preparing principals to lead schools that are successful with racially diverse students. *Educational Administration Quarterly, 40*(5), 601–632. https://doi.org/10.1177/0013161X04268839

Meiklejohn, J., Phillips, C., Freedman, M. L., Griffin, M. L., Biegel, G., Roach, A., … Saltzman, A. (2012). Integrating mindfulness training into K-12 education: Fostering the resilience of teachers and students. *Mindfulness, 3*(4), 291–307. https://doi.org/10.1007/s12671-012-0094-5

Poulin, P. A., Mackenzie, C. S., Soloway, G., & Karayolas, E. (2008). Mindfulness training as an evidenced-based approach to reducing stress and promoting well-being among human services professionals. *International Journal of Health Promotion and Education, 46,* 35–43.

Quinlan, J. R. (1990). Decision trees and decisionmaking. *IEEE. Transactions on Systems, Man, and Cybernetics, 20*(2), 339–346.

Roorda, D. L., Koomen, H. M. Y., Spilt, J. L., & Oort, F. J. (2011). The influence of affective teacher–student relationships on students' school engagement and achievement: A meta-analytic approach. *Review of Educational Research, 81*(4), 493–529. https://doi.org/10.3102/0034654311421793

Ross, R. (2013). School climate and equity. In T. Dary & T. Pickeral (Eds.), *School climate practices for implementation and sustainability: A School Climate Practice Brief, Number 1.* New York, NY: National

School Climate Center. Retrieved from www.schoolclimate.org/themes/schoolclimate/assets/pdf/practice/sc-brief-equity.pdf

Scott, S. (2004). *Fierce conversations: Achieving success at work and in life, one conversation at a time*. New York, NY: The Berkeley Publishing Group.

Singleton, G. E. (2014). *Courageous conversations about race: A field guide for achieving equity in schools* (2nd ed.). Thousand Oaks, CA: Corwin Press.

Singleton, G. E., & Linton, C. (2005). *Courageous conversations about race*. Thousand Oaks, CA: Corwin Press.

Skrla, L., McKenzie, K. B., & Scheurich, J. J. (Eds.). (2009). *Using equity audits to create equitable and excellent schools*. Thousand Oaks, CA: Corwin Press.

Skrla, L., Scheurich, J. J., Garcia, J., & Nolly, G. (2004). Equity audits: A practical leadership tool for developing equitable and excellent schools. *Educational Administration Quarterly, 40*(1), 133–161.

Stewart, T. L., Latu, I. M., Kawakami, K., & Myers, A. C. (2010). Consider the situation: Reducing automatic stereotyping through Situational Attribution Training. *Journal of Experimental Social Psychology, 46*(1), 221–225. https://doi.org/10.1016/j.jesp.2009.09.004

Sugai, G., & Horner, R. (2006). A promising approach for expanding and sustaining school-wide positive behavior suppor. *School Psychology Review, 32*(2), 245–259.

Sugai, G., Horner, R. H., Dunlap, G., Hieneman, M., Lewis, T. J., Nelson, C. M., ... Ruef, M. (2000). Applying positive behavior support and functional behavioral assessment in schools. *Journal of Positive Behavior Interventions, 2*(3), 131–143. https://doi.org/10.1177/109830070000200302

Vincent, C. G., & Tobin, T. (2010). The relationship between implementation of school-wide positive behavior support (SWPBS) and disciplinary exclusion of students from various ethnic backgrounds with and without disabilities. *Journal of Emotional and Behavioral Disorders, 19*(4), 217–232.

Yusuf, A. R., Irvine, A., & Bell, J. (2016). Reducing racial disparities in school discipline: Structured decision-making in the classroom. In R. J. Skiba, K. Mediratta, & M. K. Rausch (Eds.), *Inequality in school discipline* (pp. 99–114). New York, NY: Palgrave Macmillan US.

Zullig, K. J., Collins, R., Ghani, N., Hunter, A. A., Patton, J. M., Huebner, E. S., & Zhang, J. (2015). Preliminary development of a revised version of the School Climate Measure. *Psychological Assessment, 27*(3), 1072–1081.

Zullig, K. J., Koopman, T. M., Patton, J. M., & Ubbes, V. A. (2010). School climate: Historical review, instrument development, and school assessment. *Journal of Psychoeducational Assessment, 28*(2), 139–152. https://doi.org/10.1177/0734282909344205

What Does Implicit Bias Work Look Like?

Supporting Policy and Practice to Address Implicit Bias in Discipline

Pamela A. Fenning and Miranda B. Johnson

Introduction

Policy documents and federal guidance referencing the role of implicit bias in racial and ethnic disparities in education have proliferated in recent years (see Chapter 1). Much of this guidance focuses on the notion that implicit biases can influence decision-making and judgments about students, particularly in ambiguous or stressful situations, both of which are common decision-making constraints for PreK-12 educators and leaders (Staats, 2015). In order for PreK-12 leaders to prevent the expression of bias in schools, they need to be well versed in the conditions where implicit bias is most likely to occur in schools such as in "vulnerable decision points" or when under stress (see McIntosh, Girvan, Horner, & Smolkowski, 2014).

While research, federal policy, and advocacy literature increasingly examine the role of implicit bias in racial and ethnic disparities, practical solutions for mitigating implicit bias in school decision-making remain at an early stage of development (McIntosh et al., 2014; Osher et al., 2015; U.S. Department of Education, 2014). Our work draws heavily on a systemic effort to implement school discipline reform in one state. We offer our experiences from professional development and technical support focused on implicit bias, restorative practices, and system-wide discipline reform as a resource for PreK-12 leaders and others seeking to mitigate the impact of implicit bias on racial disproportionality in school discipline.

As our work is still evolving, significant outcome research is still needed to understand the full impact of our efforts and to inform the professional development needed to counteract the impacts of implicit bias in school settings.

Setting the Stage: School Discipline Reform in Illinois

Statewide Legislative Reform

Driven by the efforts of a youth-led advocacy organization, Voices of Youth in Chicago Education (VOYCE) and other community groups, Illinois enacted sweeping school discipline reform legislation. This legislation started with a discipline data law in 2014 and culminated in a substantive discipline reform law in 2015.

Illinois Discipline Data Law

Illinois Public Act 98–1102 (referred to in this chapter as the "Illinois Discipline Data Law") was enacted on August 26, 2014. This law requires the state education agency, the Illinois State Board of Education (ISBE), to annually compile and release data from all school districts on out-of-school suspensions (OSS), expulsions, and removal to alternative settings in lieu of another disciplinary action. The data must include all public schools in the district, including charter schools, and it must be disaggregated by race/ethnicity, gender, age, grade level, students with Limited English Proficiency (LEP in table), incident type, and discipline duration.

One hallmark of this law is that it not only requires data transparency, but also requires corrective action by districts with high rates of exclusionary discipline and racial disproportionality. School districts ranked in the top 20% of districts in the state for three consecutive years for the rate of out-of-school suspensions, expulsions without educational services, or racial/ethnic disproportionality in out-of-school suspensions and expulsions are required to develop a plan to address the identified issues. This plan must be approved at a school board meeting and posted on the district's website. Within a designated time period, the school district must submit a progress report to ISBE, including plan implementation and results (105 ILCS 5/2–3.162).

ISDR Law

Following the passage of the Illinois Discipline Data Law, Illinois enacted substantive discipline reform legislation. This legislation, Illinois Public Act 99–0456 (commonly called "SB100" in the state and which will be referred to in this chapter as "Illinois School Discipline Reform (ISDR) Law"), was signed into law on August 24, 2015 and went into effect one year later, on September 15, 2016. The ISDR Law requires school districts to minimize the use of "suspension and expulsion to the greatest extent practicable" and recommends that these exclusionary practices be used "only for legitimate educational purposes" (105 ILCS 5/10–22.6(b-5)). In addition, schools cannot use zero-tolerance policies unless otherwise mandated by law, such as federal law on weapons offenses.

The emergence of this type of statewide disciplinary reform effort has immense implications for local districts and schools. In an attempt to reduce the use of suspension and expulsion, laws such as the one in Illinois impose new limitations on the exercise of schools' discretionary authority to discipline students. For example, the ISDR Law allows school districts to assign out-of-school suspension (OSS) for three days or less "only if the student's continuing presence in school would pose a threat to school safety or a disruption to other students' learning opportunities." (105 ILCS 5/10–22.6(b-15)). For OSS

> ## Blurred Lines
>
> The ISDR Law has experienced some criticism due to vague language including: "to the greatest extent practicable," "disruption to other students' learning opportunities," and "available and appropriate interventions." Legislative language is often vague as a result of compromises to get the law passed. Typically, school officials get to define these terms, but courts may later review these. Consider avoiding vague language when writing your own school policy in order to reduce the potential of bias in subjective considerations.

of more than three days, expulsions, and disciplinary transfers to alternative schools, the standard is higher. Districts may impose these types of exclusionary discipline only if (1) "other appropriate and available behavioral and disciplinary interventions have been exhausted," and (2) the students' continuing presence in school either poses a threat to school safety or would "substantially disrupt, impede, or interfere with the operation of the school" (105 ILCS 5/10–22.6(b-15)). Further, school districts must develop a re-engagement policy for students who are suspended, expelled, or returning from alternative placement to help them make up academic work and to reintegrate into the school community.

As a key component of the interventions described in this chapter, the legislation requires districts to provide additional professional development to a range of school stakeholders. Under this law, school districts should "make reasonable efforts to provide professional development to teachers, administrators, school board members, school resource officers, and staff on the adverse consequences of school exclusion and justice-system involvement, effective classroom management strategies, culturally responsive discipline, and developmentally appropriate disciplinary methods that promote positive and healthy school climates" (105 ILCS 5/10–22.6(c-5)). The scope of the training topics and the range of district and school stakeholders identified are instructive for professional development initiatives in other states.

Did You Know?

Both authors are co-founders and inaugural members of this collaborative, which is called the *Transforming School Discipline Collaborative* (TSDC). (Please see Fenning and Johnson [2016] for more information about the formation and work of TSDC.) They are also two of the authors of TSDC's Model Student Code of Conduct and the creators of the course proposal for the collaborative's Administrators' Academy. They have traveled throughout Illinois conducting trainings for administrators and other school personnel regarding school discipline reform. They have also taught courses in the School Discipline Reform Certificate program offered by Loyola University Chicago.

Cross-Disciplinary Collaborative – Transforming School Discipline Collaborative (TSDC)

These discipline reform initiatives sparked the creation of a cross-disciplinary collaborative to support PreK-12 leaders to effectively implement school disciplinary reform. The collaborative's members include professors, attorneys, policy advocates, restorative justice practitioners, school psychologists, and community organizers. The members work in universities, legal services, non-profit organizations, civil rights advocacy organizations, and schools. TSDC adopted the following organizing principles that align with creating restorative and equitable discipline practices:

- Effectuating a positive school climate is critical to transforming disciplinary practices.
- Discipline should be prevention-oriented and build upon academic and behavioral supports for students.
- Disciplinary responses should be instructional and corrective.
- Out-of-school discipline is counterproductive and should be limited to the extent possible.

Building on these principles, the major efforts of TSDC that supported this broader framework to interrupt implicit bias and featured in this chapter are:

1. Creation and dissemination of a model student code of conduct for Illinois;
2. Creation of a discipline checklist;
3. Development of toolkits for administrators on key topics related to equitable discipline; and
4. Development and delivery of an Administrators' Academy for PreK-12 leaders focused on the implementation of state discipline legislation.

Supporting Equity in School Discipline

TSDC was formed at an opportune moment when federal and state support for establishing evidence-based and equitable discipline practices

Challenges with Change

With requirements for data reporting and suspension reduction stemming from the Every Student Succeeds Act, many states and districts will need to develop plans to comply with or enhance current equity policies. When changes are required, organizations often resist new practices. Consider implementing new policies in stages and involving key stakeholders in the decision-making process. Using shared decision-making to develop policy and implementation plans often lowers staff resistance to change. Consider who is most affected by the changes and any resources they might need to assist with responsibilities.

coincided. Following on the heels of federal guidance aimed at facilitating systemic discipline reform (U.S. Department of Education, 2014; U.S. Department of Education and Justice, 2014), the ISDR Law enacted in August 2015 required school districts to revise their school discipline policies and practices by September 2016. This timeline allowed a one-year window for districts to consider the best ways in which to effectuate school discipline reform. During this time, TSDC supported districts to begin their discipline reform process with a critical examination of district-level institutional practices, including the role of implicit bias in discipline decisions. TSDC also promoted the use of Restorative Practices in order to foster a positive school climate and the use of an instructional and corrective, rather than punitive, response to misbehaviors. (See Chapter 6 for more information on Restorative Practices.) TSDC's initiatives built upon the work of other discipline reform initiatives across the country, such as the Model Code on Education and Dignity developed by the Dignity in Schools Campaign (Dignity in Schools, 2013).

Model Student Code of Conduct

TSDC members worked together to develop a model code of conduct as a resource for use by school district leaders to ensure compliance with policy mandates under the new legislation. With the passage of the ISDR Law, TSDC members saw an opportunity to assist school districts in revising their codes of conduct to comply with the new law by adopting practices aligned with federal guidance and research on evidence-supported and equitable practices in behavior and discipline, including research on the role of implicit bias in achieving equitable discipline outcomes (Osher et al., 2015; U.S. Department of Education and Justice, 2014). The purpose of the model code is described within the document as follows:

Model Code of Conduct Major Sections

Discipline Philosophy

Rights and Responsibilities

Participation and Collaboration

Prevention, Intervention, and Disciplinary Responses

Due Process Procedures

Procedures following Suspension and Expulsion

Procedural Guidelines for Discipline of Students with Disabilities

Professional Development

Data Collection and Monitoring

> This model code is offered as a best practice of how school administrators can develop a student code of conduct that (1) is compliant with recent changes to Illinois law and (2) advances the goal of fairness and equity in the discipline process. In some places, the model code goes beyond the strict requirements of current law to encompass the intent behind legislative reforms to reduce the use of exclusionary school discipline. Achieving the purpose of the legislation requires a fundamental shift in school climate and policies to a prevention-oriented and student-centered approach that keeps students in school, fully engaged and on track to graduate.
>
> (TSDC, 2016, p. 1)

After a core team of TSDC steering committee members drafted the model code of conduct, key constituents including school administrators, school psychologists, school attorneys, parent advocates, and state education agency personnel had the opportunity to provide feedback before the draft was finalized. (The Model Code of Conduct is available via a link in this book's online resources.)

The model code of conduct is structured with "blue boxes" that contain information about best practices in the field and legislative mandates that TSDC members suggest districts consider in drafting language for each section. The boxed text below is an example of a "blue box," featuring examples on disciplinary guidance. Suggested language is provided that districts can include in their own disciplinary codes when suitable for a district's philosophy, school climate, and perspective. (Please see Fenning and Johnson [2016] for more information related to the development and components of the model code as part of a comprehensive discipline policy.)

Disciplinary Philosophy

Before developing your district or school's code of conduct, it is important to first come to a consensus about your discipline philosophy. The discipline philosophy that this model code articulates is a positive vision based on best practices, research, and experiences of communities. The discipline philosophy sets the tone for the climate of the district or school and should be aligned with other systems and practices that support all students to stay in school, learn, and be successful.

Developing your district or school's discipline philosophy presents a meaningful opportunity for the educational community to engage in a collaborative process that results in a commitment to a shared vision. Your district or school should carefully consider how this process can be inclusive of voices often underrepresented in these decisions, particularly the students and families that tend to be most impacted and excluded by the discipline system. The sections [provided in the model code] are examples of what can be produced with input and collaboration from key constituents, particularly students, families and teachers.

(TSDC Model Student Code of Conduct, 2016, citing Dignity in Schools, 2013, and Schriber, Horn, Peter, Bellinger, & Fischer, 2017)

The model code also incorporates a one-page diagram containing a suggested approach to student behaviors (see Figure 7.1). This diagram

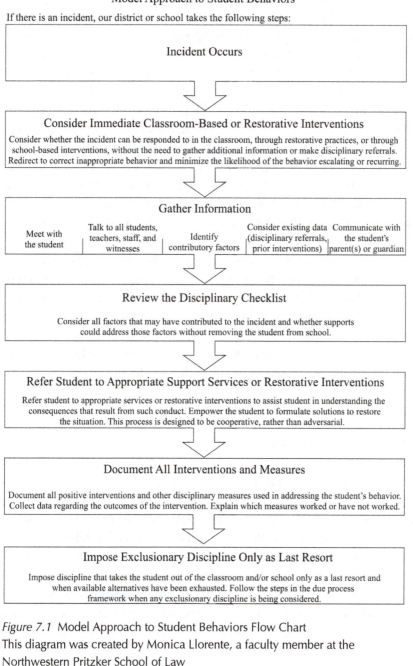

Model Approach to Student Behaviors

If there is an incident, our district or school takes the following steps:

Incident Occurs

Consider Immediate Classroom-Based or Restorative Interventions

Consider whether the incident can be responded to in the classroom, through restorative practices, or through school-based interventions, without the need to gather additional information or make disciplinary referrals. Redirect to correct inappropriate behavior and minimize the likelihood of the behavior escalating or recurring.

Gather Information

| Meet with the student | Talk to all students, teachers, staff, and witnesses | Identify contributory factors | Consider existing data (disciplinary referrals, prior interventions) | Communicate with the student's parent(s) or guardian |

Review the Disciplinary Checklist

Consider all factors that may have contributed to the incident and whether supports could address those factors without removing the student from school.

Refer Student to Appropriate Support Services or Restorative Interventions

Refer student to appropriate services or restorative interventions to assist student in understanding the consequences that result from such conduct. Empower the student to formulate solutions to restore the situation. This process is designed to be cooperative, rather than adversarial.

Document All Interventions and Measures

Document all positive interventions and other disciplinary measures used in addressing the student's behavior. Collect data regarding the outcomes of the intervention. Explain which measures worked or have not worked.

Impose Exclusionary Discipline Only as Last Resort

Impose discipline that takes the student out of the classroom and/or school only as a last resort and when available alternatives have been exhausted. Follow the steps in the due process framework when any exclusionary discipline is being considered.

Figure 7.1 Model Approach to Student Behaviors Flow Chart
This diagram was created by Monica Llorente, a faculty member at the Northwestern Pritzker School of Law
Source: Model Student Code of Conduct (TSDC, 2016)

is intended to illustrate how schools and districts can make clear to all school stakeholders the process for making exclusionary school discipline a "last resort" option. The suggested approach begins with a requirement to first utilize immediate and restorative interventions within the classroom prior to removing a student from class. Once a student is removed, then the suggested approach is to systematically gather information from relevant people, including the student, the parent or guardian, the student's teachers, and any eyewitnesses. Gathering information from the parent or guardian prior to the issuance of a school suspension is an important step, because it provides an opportunity for the parent to provide information on potential student-level factors resulting in the student's behavior, such as bullying, family separation, or homelessness. Often schools and districts speak with parents after the discipline decision has already been made, which increases the likelihood of a conflictual, rather than collaborative, relationship between the school and the parent. TSDC's approach to student behaviors is designed to help schools identify and exhaust appropriate and available interventions designed to address the root causes of the student behavior (Osher et al., 2015) and to thereby reduce reliance on school suspension and expulsion. Embedded within this approach to student behaviors is a discipline checklist intended to help schools and districts to reduce ambiguity and subjectivity in disciplinary decisions that may lead to bias.

Discipline Checklist

The discipline checklist contains questions aligned with a problem-solving process school teams could use to determine appropriate interventions and decide whether an offense merits a suspension. Sample guiding questions adapted from the full discipline checklist are presented in Table 7.1. These sample questions show how school districts may take a structured, systematic, and restorative approach to implement the ISDR Law. A structured decision-making process is particularly important in suspension decisions involving subjective offenses in which implicit biases may shape outcomes (McIntosh et al., 2014) and result in racial and ethnic disproportionality (Skiba et al., 2011; Skiba, Michael, Nardo, & Peterson, 2002). Given that state law in Illinois, like many states, allows for students to be suspended

Table 7.1 Guiding Questions to Structure Decisions around Suspension

Questions	Guidelines	Considerations
Would the student's continuing presence in school cause a threat to school safety or a disruption to other students' learning opportunities?	Short-term suspensions are *only* allowed if the student's continuing presence in school would pose a threat to school safety or a disruption to other students' learning opportunities.	School staff should be particularly mindful of this standard when imposing out-of-school discipline for offense categories that rely principally on the subjective interpretation of school staff (e.g., insubordinate behavior, defiance, disobedience, or disrespect).
	Our district or school maintains a protocol to determine whether a student poses a threat to school safety or would disrupt the operation of the school. The determination of safety threats is based only on actual risks and objective evidence (see Cornell & Sheras, 2006) and not on stereotypes or generalizations. (U.S. Department of Health and Human Services, 2016).	In making the determination as to whether suspension or expulsion is warranted, school staff should consider the following factors: The conduct at issue, the root cause of the conduct and whether it has been addressed; Age of the student and ability to understand consequences; Capability of the student to carry out the threat; Student's discipline history and the frequency of inappropriate behavior; Credibility of the student and willingness to acknowledge his or her behavior; and Effect of the conduct on the school environment.

Note: Excerpted and adapted from TSDC Model Student Code of Conduct (2016).

out-of-school if their presence in school poses a threat to school safety or a disruption to other students' learning, creating clear definitions and protocols at the school or district level to define these terms and relevant factors to consider is important to ensure equitable decision-making. Table 7.1 provides an example of how a district could define parameters for school staff to make decisions based on subjective standards from state law like "threat to school safety" and "disruption to other students' learning opportunities."

Implicit biases are more likely to affect behavior in ambiguous and stressful situations (Staats, 2015; Staats, Capatosto, Wright, & Jackson, 2016). McIntosh and colleagues (2014) recommended that educators determine when they are in the midst of a "vulnerable decision point," such as when a teacher decides whether to refer a student to the office or an administrator makes a determination to suspend a student. When reaching a vulnerable decision point, practicing a "neutralizing routine" can potentially mitigate implicit biases. A neutralizing routine can be something as simple as delaying a conversation with the student until after class or taking a few deep breaths before making a quick and in-the-moment decision (McIntosh, Hill, & Coccimiglio, 2015). Given that implicit biases are out of school staff's conscious control (Staats, 2015; Staats et al., 2016), having a systematic discipline checklist may help to make automatic associations more explicit (Devine, 1989) and thereby help mitigate the effects of implicit bias in deciding whether to suspend a student. Requiring school staff to detail their rationale for using out-of-school discipline through the use of a checklist also helps to ensure that decisions to use exclusionary discipline are thoroughly documented and that alternative forms of intervention have been considered.

In order to mitigate the impact of implicit bias on decision-making, TSDC's discipline checklist includes several questions aimed at establishing new default rules for schools and districts. Suggested default rules include prohibiting suspension and expulsion for a first-time offense and imposing grade-level restrictions on suspension and expulsion except in certain specified circumstances. While neither of these provisions are expressly required by state or federal law, adopting a default rule against exclusion in certain circumstances requires district personnel to first look to non-exclusionary alternatives when imposing consequences for misbehavior and means that they have to document their reasons when they deviate from the standard rule. It also means that there can be simplified communication of district policy to school personnel, parents, and students. For example, a district that adopted restrictions on suspensions and expulsions for first-time offenses could announce, "In general, our district does not believe in suspensions or expulsions for first-time offenses. We believe in second chances and in teaching our students the behavior we expect of them." Such a policy is easy to communicate, reduces the likelihood of bias in deciding which students deserve a second chance, and still allows for deviations for unusual and serious circumstances.

Implicit Bias Language

To further attend to implicit bias, TSDC's model code specifically addressed the need for implicit bias training beyond the general recommendations in the discipline legislation. Such training is required by the ISDR Law provision that districts provide

A Sample Default Rule for First-Time Offenses

TSDC's Disciplinary Checklist asks, "Has the student previously violated the school code?" and provides the following suggested language:

A suspension of more than three days or expulsion cannot be imposed for a first-time offense. The district and school must have first implemented other behavioral interventions and followed the district and school process for documenting when these interventions have been "exhausted." Exceptions to these policies can be made in exigent or emergency circumstances involving school safety with justification and approval by the superintendent or a designee, together with a showing that there were no appropriate and available interventions.

The first draft of the Discipline Checklist in the TSDC Model Student Code of Conduct (2016) was created by Rachel Bonnette, a 2015 graduate of Loyola University Chicago School of Law.

professional development on culturally responsive discipline practices (see Chapter 6), and it is also recommended by the U.S. Department of Education (2014). The model code suggests that each district and school have a professional development plan "to ensure that all staff members have the tools, skills and support that they need to implement [its] discipline policy" and that the

> Where appropriate, schools may choose to explore using cultural competence training to enhance staff awareness of their implicit or unconscious biases and the harms associated with using or failing to counter racial and ethnic stereotypes.
>
> (U.S. Department of Education, *Guiding Principles: A Resource Guide for Improving School Climate and Discipline*, 2014)

plan be reviewed and revised annually. The model code includes implicit bias training as one of the areas of training required and also specifically names key stakeholders who may need support when managing student behavior across multiple school contexts, such as teachers, bus drivers, cafeteria staff, security officers, school resource officers, and administrators.

Toolkit

> These toolkits are available on the Transforming School Discipline Collaborative website at www.transformschooldiscipline.org/

TSDC members developed toolkits on topics related to exclusionary discipline and disproportionality included as part of the Administrators' Academy. Topics include: restorative justice, effective functional analysis of behaviors and behavior interventions, parent engagement, and school discipline in charter schools. TSDC continues to develop and expand this toolkit based on identified needs of school stakeholders. For example, TSDC has included a "district spotlight" as part of a regular newsletter in order to showcase the positive changes that schools and districts are making in their approach to student behaviors. In addition, TSDC is working on a racial bias and discipline disproportionality toolkit for administrators.

Administrators' Academy

To support the implementation of reforms to school discipline practices, TSDC developed and delivered an Administrators' Academy, a day-long professional development workshop approved by Illinois State Board of

Education. To retain their licensure in Illinois, administrators must annually attend an Administrators' Academy, so the collaborative identified this existing training requirement as an opportunity to provide training to administrators on prevention-oriented approaches to school discipline. TSDC developed a three-pronged cross-disciplinary approach focused on training administrators in the following areas:

1. Research on exclusionary discipline and root cause analysis;
2. Restorative Practices; and
3. Changes to ISDR Law.

The goal of the training is to facilitate a transition from a punitive to a restorative mindset in addressing common student misbehavior and to provide administrators with additional tools and skills to reform school discipline practices in their schools and districts. During the Administrators' Academy, a school psychologist or special education administrator, a restorative justice practitioner, and an attorney deliver separate and interconnected segments.

In advance of the training, participants are asked to complete a data worksheet for their school or district describing the top three behaviors leading to suspensions and expulsions, as well as providing discipline data in the aggregate and disaggregated by race/ethnicity and special education status (worksheet available with online book content). Participants are also asked to read the book *Closing the Discipline Gap* (Losen, 2015) and are provided a Google drive of supplementary resources, including documents on implicit bias, federal school discipline guidance, text of the ISDR Law, and relevant TSDC toolkits.

Trainings begin with a presentation on the research and data that supported reducing the use of exclusionary discipline. In particular, the presentation highlights the negative impacts of school suspension and expulsion on students, the long-standing disproportionality in exclusionary discipline, the importance of addressing implicit bias as it relates to school discipline decision-making, and evidence-supported strategies for addressing student misbehavior. The next portion of the presentation focuses on guiding participants through a case study example of a root cause analysis (based on Osher et al., 2015). Participants are then divided into groups to identify the root cause of a common behavior driving school discipline in their buildings. Many participants identify classroom disruption, insubordination, and defiance as the most common offenses resulting in out-of-school suspensions in their schools and districts. Once they identify a particular behavior, participants are asked to describe what their schools or districts were already doing to address the behavior and to identify specific action steps that they could take to address the behavior in the future. The facilitator asks the participants to identify supports in each of three tiers: Tier 1 (universal supports that they would provide to all students), Tier 2 (supports provided to students identified as at risk) consistent with a multi-tiered system of support (MTSS) approach (McIntosh & Goodman, 2016), and Tier 3 (services provided to students most in need of support). Participants are then invited to share the behavior that they identified and their action steps with the larger group.

The second portion of the training focuses on the use of restorative practices. The main goals of this segment are to: (1) help participants understand the difference between punitive accountability and restorative accountability, (2) build their understanding of key terms and types of restorative practices, (3) develop skills in asking restorative questions, and (4) support action planning to implement restorative practices. The facilitator uses a combination of formats, including presentation, facilitated dialogue, activities, and working group discussion. The restorative justice segment is two-and-a-half hours, the longest part of the six hours of curricular instruction provided at the workshop. The session spans the lunch hour, with a presentation and facilitated activity typically taking place prior to lunch, and an activity and working group discussion taking place after lunch.

The last portion of the training is a presentation on legal mandates related to school discipline. This portion of the training is intentionally placed last, so that participants are not focused on legal compliance but rather on how to implement school discipline reform with a restorative and equity focus. The members of the TSDC training team realized that once participants had internalized the reasons for undertaking school discipline reform, they better understood the purpose behind the legal mandates and approached the changes in the law with a greater openness to making systemic change. As such, this portion of the training focuses on major changes to ISDR Law, implementation strategies and questions, and short exercises requiring participants to share in pairs or write down strategies for implementing the legal mandates based on the content of earlier presentations. The legal portion culminates with a series of hypothetical student examples that require participants to apply the disciplinary approach discussed earlier.

At the end of the day, participants complete an individual activity in which they are required to write or revise a discipline procedure to address a major behavior challenge in their school or district. A sample activity is available on the companion website for this book. The purpose of this culminating activity is to help participants integrate their learning from the one-day workshop by immediately applying the material to a school or district policy or procedure. The activity is also intended to give administrators a takeaway from the workshop that they could immediately bring back to their school or district team to consider for possible implementation.

At the conclusion of the workshop, the facilitators bring participants back together to discuss key takeaways from the day. Participants are asked to take out their calendars and write down one immediate action step based on the content covered within the training, such as reading the resources provided in the Google drive, sharing one or more of the resources with a school or district team for discussion, or reaching out to an outside trainer to do professional development for their school or district teams. The goal of this final activity is to help ensure that the momentum gained during the workshop continues beyond the one-day training.

As of May 2018, TSDC has delivered 25 Administrators' Academies to over 800 participants across the state of Illinois. These Administrators' Academies were delivered in a variety of formats, including: (1) all participants in attendance from one specific district, (2) participants from multiple districts attending through a regional office of education or an intermediate service center, and (3) participants from multiple districts working with the same special education cooperative. Loyola University Chicago continues to evaluate outcomes from the Administrators' Academies through a content analysis of the products generated by workshop participants and through interviews.

Lessons Learned

Throughout the process of delivering the Administrators' Academies and related trainings, the TSDC team learned a number of lessons and made changes to the

> The importance of discussing reasons for implicit bias training to educators is further discussed in the following chapter.

curriculum accordingly. An initial lesson learned was the importance of explaining why implicit bias had been identified as a key explanatory variable for disproportionality in school suspensions and expulsions. In an attempt to shorten the presentation, an earlier version of the training referred to implicit bias as an important area of focus for school discipline reform work but removed compelling research ruling out student behavioral severity as accounting for racial discipline disparities. The facilitators later learned that some participants continued to have the mistaken belief that racial disproportionality in school discipline was explained by differences in student behavior. As a result, the training team increased the amount of time being devoted to explicitly addressing implicit bias and explaining why the research had substantively ruled out other potential explanatory variables for explaining racial/ethnic disparities in suspensions and expulsions, such as differences in behavioral severity, poverty, and approaches to calculating disproportionality. Content based on the work of Staats and colleagues (2016) was added to the professional development with a focus on helping participants understand how implicit associations could unconsciously influence information processing. This approach helped to increase the receptivity of participants to planning implicit bias training for their staff and teachers and to consider incorporating the use of a systematic problem-solving tool like the checklist featured in this chapter.

In addition, the training team adapted the root cause analysis activity after noticing that participants were arriving at reasons for discipline that were internal to students and families (e.g., poverty, gangs and violence in the neighborhood), rather than school factors that were in the school/district control to address. This tendency to attribute student behaviors to factors internal to students and families was inadvertently contributing to a deficit-thinking model of student behavior (Walker, 2011). In order to address this, the team found that it was helpful to ask participants to problem-solve root causes of school discipline by using a series of probing questions aimed at identifying school factors, particularly those that were relational in nature. Based on this observation, the facilitator introduced the root cause analysis by using guiding questions and principles promoting a "growth mindset" versus a fixed mindset (Dweck, 2008) that were integrated into a handout adapted from the professional development materials and experiences of the Umoja Student Development Corporation, an agency member on the TSDC steering committee and a training partner along with the team in several of the Administrators' Academies. These questions are adapted from the Umoja Student Development Corporation's Disciplinary Intervention Curriculum (Dworin, 2015):

1. As you begin reviewing data, describe only what you see. Do not leap to conclusions or interpretations. Express what you do and do not see in the form of non-judgmental questions or statements. (For example: "I see that 25% of the discipline referrals are referrals of African American freshman students for insubordination.")

2. Analyze and discuss data with a growth mindset (Dweck, 2008), not a fixed mindset. Ask questions like: How can these data help me to best support students and teachers? How can I change my/the school's practice based on these data? Explaining data results based on internal student and family demographics is not likely to support a growth mindset (e.g., students face high rates of poverty).

3. Analyze and discuss data through a restorative framework rather than using it to shame or criminalize others.

4. Surface the lenses, biases, and experiences that may impact how you view and explain the data.

(Dworin, 2015)

In formulating these questions, TSDC additionally drew upon work in the dropout literature, which has documented the important role of relationship-driven interventions rather than focusing on student internal attributes in facilitating student engagement and keeping students in school (Anderson, Christenson, Sinclair, & Lehr, 2004).

Another lesson learned was the importance of keeping the training as interactive as possible. Given that the training team brings together trainers with expertise in different disciplines, trainers frequently relied on lecture as a primary modality of instruction in order to help participants learn the core content. As a result, presentations were sometimes longer than the activity portions. As time went on, the training team reduced the amount of PowerPoint™ slides presented, choosing to instead prioritize training time to address key concepts, provide an opportunity to practice skills like restorative conversations, and engage in working group time to meaningfully address how the concepts presented related to each participant's school or district.

The TSDC team increasingly recognized the importance of specifically focusing on the needs of students with disabilities. Consistent with the national literature, there remains significant disproportionality of discipline of students with disabilities (U.S. Department of Education, 2016). Many school districts faced difficulties in integrating the ISDR Law with the federal and state procedural protections relating to discipline with disabilities, so the collaborative added a segment to the legal portion of the training that particularly focused on that intersection. In addition, because data showed that students with disabilities who were Black were particularly vulnerable to OSS, the collaborative included research relating to the intersectionality of disparities among students with multiple identities – particularly special education needs and race/ethnicity (Capatosto, 2015).

Another lesson learned was the value of presenting to school and district teams from a single district. When Administrators' Academies were offered on-site at a particular district and brought together teams of school leaders, the trainers could present teams with a root cause analysis activity that used the district's own data. Teams found enormous value in having outside facilitators present key areas of consideration based on their review of the district's own policies and data. In addition, because working groups were composed of various school leaders who were accustomed to working together, they were able to engage more quickly in constructive problem-solving using the tools that the trainers presented. When it was not possible to present the trainings on-site at a single district, TSDC found it was helpful to incentivize the participation of multiple members of a school or district team by offering a discount for multiple attendees from a single district. Having a critical mass of school leaders attend the training allowed the schools and districts to operationalize the training better than they could when only a single person attended the training.

Initial Outcomes of School Discipline Reform Efforts

TSDC's efforts in Illinois represented one component of a statewide discipline reform process impacting over 800 school districts across the state. Therefore, it is instructive to look at the statewide picture following the implementation of school discipline reform efforts in Illinois. Following the passage (2015–2016 school year) and the first year in which the ISDR

Table 7.2 Data Snapshot: Before and After School Discipline Reform in Illinois

Type of Disciplinary Action	Prior to Reform (2014–15)	After Passage (2015–16)	Reform Year 1 (2016–17)
Expulsion – received educational services	498	461	380
Expulsion – did not receive educational services	637	216	155
In-school suspension	189,203	170,156	163,263
Out-of-school suspension	148,086	124,361	98,043
Transfers to alternative schools in lieu of another disciplinary action	1,558	1,234	1,788

Source: Illinois State Board of Education, End of Year Student Discipline Reports (2014–15, 2015–16, and 2016–17)

Law went into effect (2016–2017 school year), there has been an overall statewide reduction in suspensions and expulsions. As Table 7.2 shows, the total numbers of expulsions, in-school suspensions, and OSS went down in the year following the passage of the ISDR Law, even prior to the law going into effect. The total number of suspensions and expulsions went down further in the school year following the law's effective date (September 2016). While controlled statistical analyses are needed to substantiate these findings, the initial descriptive data available suggests that increased emphasis across the state on the importance of reducing the use of exclusionary discipline aligned with the ISDR Law coincided with district-reported reductions in the use of suspension and expulsion. Of note in these data is the increase in the use of disciplinary transfers to alternative schools in the 2016–2017 school year, suggesting that some districts may be increasingly relying on alternative school transfers instead of expelling students.

When taking a closer look at OSS data disaggregated by race and ethnicity, the number of districts reporting OSS for all racial/ethnic subgroups decreased (see Table 7.3). However, racial disproportionality of suspensions with respect to African American/Black students has persisted

Table 7.3 Out-of-School Suspensions: Before and After School Discipline Reform in Illinois

Out-of-School Suspension (% of student population)	Prior to Reform (2014–15)	After Passage (2015–16)	Reform Year 1 (2016–17)
Hispanic or Latino (25–26%)	26,443 (17.9%)	22,342 (18.0%)	17,179 (17.5%)
Black or African American (17–18)	74,731 (50.5%)	63,751 (51.3%)	53,301 (54.4%)
White (48–49%)	39,780 (26.9%)	31,762 (25.5%)	22,212 (22.7%)
Two or More Races (3%)	5,823 (3.9%)	5,446 (4.4%)	4,519 (4.6%)
Asian (5%)	764 (0.5%)	632 (0.5%)	496 (0.5%)
Native Hawaiian or Other Pacific Islander (<1%)	109 (0.1%)	67 (0.1%)	54 (0.1%)
American Indian or Alaskan Native (<1%)	436 (0.3%)	361 (0.3%)	282 (0.3%)
Total	**148,086**	**124,361**	**98,043**

Source: Illinois State Board of Education End of Year Student Discipline Reports and Fall Enrollment Counts (2014–15, 2015–16, and 2016–17)

since the enactment of the ISDR Law. Even in the school year following the implementation of the law (the 2016–2017 school year), Black students accounted for over half of OSS in Illinois, even though they are only about 17% of the state K-12 enrollment. These findings show the continued importance of using a race equity lens when implementing school discipline reform. While the TSDC trainings did adopt such an approach, neither the ISDR Law nor the majority of the trainings offered throughout the state included an explicit focus on racial disproportionality in school discipline and strategies to reduce disproportionality.

In general, a major challenge facing the implementation of school discipline reform in Illinois is insufficient training and professional development with all school stakeholders, particularly teachers, in alternatives to exclusionary discipline. In a report documenting findings from a survey of teachers following implementation of school discipline reform in

Illinois, teachers reported that the districts provided them with limited and unsatisfactory training to help them implement the new law (Teach Plus, 2018). Teachers also reported that districts took inadequate steps to replace suspensions and expulsions with other types of interventions and consequences. The report recommended strengthening legislative language to (1) require districts to provide thorough training on the ISDR Law, (2) require implementation of disciplinary practices informed by restorative justice and trauma-informed approaches, (3) ensure ongoing support and consistency for teachers in implementing discipline reform, and (4) provide adequate funding and accountability mechanisms for districts relating to compliance with school discipline reform. As a result of these findings and the experience throughout the state, policy advocacy and community organizations are working with legislators to strengthen state legislation. Future efforts will focus on continued evaluation of the ISDR Law and directing efforts to advocate for more professional development and technical assistance to educators in implementing evidence-supported and promising alternatives to exclusionary school discipline.

Conclusions

TSDC's efforts to date capitalized on state-level discipline reform to impact the development and administrative oversight of discipline policies and practices. One function of TSDC was to increase attention on the issue of implicit bias in discipline decision-making in an effort to create sustained changes. However, the use of exclusionary discipline and racial inequities in its administration remains deeply embedded in school culture and practices. Accordingly, discipline reform efforts should be viewed as long-term school change processes that require structured and sustained professional development and monitoring. Further work remains necessary to fully understand how to apply emerging research on implicit bias to change racial/ethnic disparities in education, particularly in the use of exclusionary discipline. This statewide collaborative effort to help PreK-12 leaders, schools, and districts create more equitable and prevention-oriented discipline policies and practices provides a potential strategy for others who are doing similar work and embarking on large-scale systemic reform processes.

References

Anderson, A. R., Christenson, S. L., Sinclair, M. F., & Lehr, C. A. (2004). Check & Connect: The importance of relationships for promoting engagement with school. *Journal of School Psychology, 42*, 95–113. doi:10.1016/j.jsp.2004.01.002

Capatosto, K. (2015). *Ohio discipline data: An analysis of ability and race.* Retrieved from http://kirwaninstitute.osu.edu/wp-content/uploads/2016/04/Ohio-Discipline-Data-An-Analysis-of-Ability-and-Race.pdf

Devine, P. G. (1989). Stereotypes and prejudice: Their automatic and controlled components. *Journal of Personality and Social Psychology, 56*(1), 5–18.

Dignity in Schools. (2013). *A model code on education and dignity.* Retrieved from www.dignityinschools.org/our-work/model-school-code

Dweck, C. (2008). *Mindset: The new psychology of success.* New York, NY: Random House.

Dworin, S-B (Ed.). (2015). *Disciplinary intervention curriculum.* Chicago, IL: Umoja Student Development Corporation. Retrieved from http://store.umojacorporation.org/

Fenning, P., & Johnson, M. (2016). Developing prevention-oriented discipline codes of conduct. *Children's Legal Rights Journal, 36*(2), 107–136.

Illinois General Assembly (eff. Aug. 26, 2014). Public Act 98–1102. Retrieved from www.ilga.gov/legislation/publicacts/fulltext.asp?Name=098-1102.

Illinois General Assembly (eff. Sep. 15, 2016). Public Act 99–0456. Retrieved from www.ilga.gov/legislation/publicacts/fulltext.asp?Name=099-0456

Illinois State Board of Education, Fall Enrollment Counts (2014–2015, 2015–16, and 2016–17). Retrieved from www.isbe.net/Pages/Fall-Enrollment-Counts.aspx

Illinois State Board of Education, End of Year Student Discipline Reports (2014–2015, 2015–16, and 2016–17). Retrieved from www.isbe.net/Pages/Expulsions-Suspensions-and-Truants-by-District.aspx.

Losen, D. (Ed.). (2015). *Closing the school discipline gap: Equitable remedies for excessive exclusion.* New York, NY: Teacher College Press.

McIntosh, K., & Goodman, S. (2016). *Integrated multi-tiered systems of support blending RTI and PBIS.* New York, NY: Guilford Press.

McIntosh, K., Girvan, E. J., Horner, R. B., & Smolkowski, K. (2014). Education not incarceration: A conceptual model for reducing racial and ethnic disproportionality in school discipline. *Journal of Applied Research on Children, 5*(2), Article 4, 1–22.

McIntosh, K., Hill, B., & Coccimiglio, S. (2015). *Reducing the effects of implicit bias in school discipline.* Retrieved from www.pbis.org/Common/Cms/files/Forum15_Presentations/C4_McIntosh-et-al.pdf

Osher, D., Fisher, D. Amos, L, Katz, J., Dwyer, K., Duffey, T., & Colombi, G. D. (2015). *Addressing the root causes of disparities in school discipline: An educator's action planning guide.* Washington, DC: National Center on Safe Supportive Learning Environments (Support and Collaboration with United States Department of Education).

Schriber, S., Horn, S. S., Peter, C., Bellinger, L. B., & Fischer, D. (2017). Supporting LGB/T youth: Comprehensive school transformation as effective bullying prevention. In S. T. Russell, & S. Horn (Eds.), *Sexual orientation, gender identity, and schooling: The nexus of research, practice, and policy* (pp. 75–96). London, UK: Oxford University Press.

Skiba, J. S., Michael, R. S., Nardo, A. C., & Peterson, R. L. (2002). The color of discipline: Sources of racial and gender disproportionality in school punishment. *Urban Review, 34*(4), 317–342.

Skiba, R. J., Horner, R. H., Choong-Geun, C., Rausch, M. K., May, S. L., & Tobin, T. (2011). Race is not neutral: A national investigation of African American and Latino disproportionality in school discipline. *School Psychology Review, 40*, 85–107.

Staats, C. (2015). Understanding implicit bias: What educators should know. *American Educator, 39*(4), 29–43. Retrieved from www.aft.org/ae/winter2015-2016/staats

Staats, C., Capatosto, K., Wright, R. A., & Jackson, V. W. (2016). State of the science: Implicit bias review. Kirwan Institute for the Study of Race and Ethnicity. Columbus, OH: The Ohio State University.

Teach Plus. (2018). *From zero to SB100: Teachers' views on implementation of school discipline reform.* Boston, MA: Teach Plus. Retrieved from https://teachplus.org/sites/default/files/publication/pdf/from_zero_to_sb100-_teachers_views_on_implementation_of_school_discipline_reform_final.pdf

TSDC. (2016). *TSDC's model student code of conduct: An interdisciplinary approach to transforming school discipline.* Retrieved from www.isbe.net/documents/tsdc-model-code-conduct.pdf

TSDC. (n.d.) Transforming School Discipline Collaborative. Retrieved from www.transformschooldiscipline.org/

U.S. Department of Education. (2014). *Guiding principles: A resource guide for improving school climate and discipline*. Washington, DC. Retrieved from www2.ed.gov/policy/gen/guid/school-discipline/guiding-principles.pdf.

U.S. Department of Education. (2016). Office of Special Education and Rehabilitative Services. Dear Colleague Letter on the Inclusion of Behavior Supports in Individualized Education Programs. Retrieved from www2.ed.gov/policy/gen/guide/school-discipline/files/dcl-on-pbis-in-ieps-08-01-2016.pdf

U.S. Department of Education and Justice. (2014, Jan 8). *Joint "dear colleague" letter*. Washington, DC. Retrieved from www2.ed.gov/about/offices/list/ocr/letters/colleague-201401-title-vi.html

Walker, K. L. (2011). Deficit thinking and the effective teacher. *Education and Urban Society, 43*(5), 576–597.

8 Conducting a Successful Implicit Bias Training

Kimberly Barsamian Kahn

Introduction

Implicit bias trainings have become prevalent across domains and industries, particularly over the last five to ten years. From educational systems to healthcare and Fortune 500 companies, organizations are recognizing the importance and impact that implicit bias can have on their employees and constituents. Indeed, many organizations and college campuses now employ a Chief Diversity Officer or Vice President of Diversity, whose duties often include addressing implicit bias. As this book has highlighted, implicit bias interventions must be broadly implemented. That is, achieving long-term changes within a setting necessitates a multi-faceted and multi-level approach to implicit bias, including individual-level training, organizational-level changes, and policy implementation and/or remediation. As part of this larger strategy, implicit bias trainings, in which implicit bias is explained while providing strategies to counteract bias to the training audience, are an important piece. However, they are only one piece in what must be a larger strategy, and one training alone will likely not be sufficient to fully reduce implicit bias within a setting. That said, implicit bias trainings can play a role in establishing the foundation, buy-in, and motivation to change implicit bias among individuals and organizations.

Chapter Focus

This chapter focuses on implicit bias trainings, specifically, as one piece in a broader strategy to reduce implicit bias within a setting. How do you structure and deliver an implicit bias training? What pieces of advice are there for organizations interested in this type of training? This chapter provides practical suggestions for developing and implementing implicit bias training interventions, with a focus on schools and similar organizational structures. Notes from past training experiences, key points to emphasize, and lessons learned are discussed to aid practitioners who are interested in addressing implicit bias in their organizations.

About the Author and Team

This advice comes from academic experts on implicit bias who have conducted bias trainings across industries and organizations. My collaborators (e.g., Dr. Phillip Atiba Goff, Dr. Jack Glaser, researchers with the Gender, Race, and Sexual Prejudice lab at Portland State University, and others) and I have published empirical studies on implicit bias, developing and expanding both the theoretical and practical basis for unconscious bias, and spoken internationally as recognized experts on this topic. We have also created and delivered implicit bias trainings to organizations including schools, work companies, and police departments. While trainings should be tailored to the specific organization, as discussed below, many key lessons and similarities emerge across contexts. For more information on trainings, please see my past publications and writings (e.g., Kahn, Goff, & Glaser, 2016). This chapter now turns to the development of implicit bias trainings and how to get started.

Planning an Implicit Bias Training: Pre-Implementation Phase

Your organization or school has decided to implement an implicit bias training. You might be asking, "Now what do I do?" There are a variety of ways to begin and decisions to be made in the planning process. Here are some tips toward developing a successful training, starting from these initial planning stages.

Establishing Support

First, it is imperative that the training program has buy-in and explicit support from all leadership levels. This is an essential part that will impact the viability and success of the training. Support should come in the form of outward endorsement through messages, and involvement in the decision-making and development process, as well as follow up both during and after the training with members and others in leadership positions. As discussed earlier, implicit bias training should be one piece in a larger organization-wide intervention strategy, so this leadership support should, hopefully, already be in place when training is added. If an implicit bias training is going to occur at an earlier stage in the process, more time should be devoted to building support during long-term strategy development planning.

Choosing the Trainer

Next, one must consider who is going to conduct the training. Collaborating with training experts and key stakeholders both in and outside the organization is a highly successful strategy. There are many academic experts and trainers in implicit bias that one can hire to deliver a training to a school or organization. The benefits of this approach are its relative ease on the organization, having an established and vetted training, and a set curriculum. Having an expert involved at some level, whether it is for guidance, consultation, and/or delivering the training itself, is a highly recommended step. Academic experts on implicit bias trainings can provide the most up-to-date scientific information in a field that is constantly growing and developing, which enhances the training's legitimacy. Other times, organizations may want to develop their own training, which can then be tailored to the local context. This may involve organization members or collaborators taking the lead on the development and delivery of the training. The benefits of this approach are that the training can come from an in-house person with built-in legitimacy who may address unique aspects and the history of the organization.

A hybrid approach that involves collaboration between content experts and local stakeholders is a recommended approach. Having both parties work together cooperatively, regardless of who is delivering the final training or which group is taking the lead, allows for the benefits of both the scientific background and the local expertise. Both groups can jointly develop and discuss the training through meetings and working sessions. Indeed, the collaborative development process itself, with key stakeholders on both sides engaging in the material, can be part of the intervention strategy within an organization, increasing buy-in and engagement.

When considering how to deliver the training, several options are also available. Having an academic expert team provide the training again provides scientific knowledge and legitimacy, but lacks the internal reputation and trust. Conversely, an internal person or team may suffer from the perceived lack of knowledge. This is why it is important to have an expert involved in the collaborative development process if the plan is to have the training delivered by an internal member. Another common model is a "train the trainer" approach, where a small group of individuals within an organization is trained on the material, and the trainers then deliver the training to larger groups in the organization. In this model, having the trainers work collaboratively with academic experts is a useful step. Finally, another possibility is to employ a joint team for the training administration, in which an academic expert is paired with an internal member to conduct the training. This pairing in the training itself offers both the scientific expertise for more technical questions, as well as practical and more context-specific knowledge. Which model is right for your specific organization will depend on the organization's goals, resources, access, and time available.

Understanding the Context

It is key to develop intervention materials that are specific to the context, regardless of the training set-up. For this pre-training development stage, spending time determining the needs of the particular context is recommended. What has led this organization to want an implicit bias training? What kinds of diversity or other related trainings does the organization already conduct? What are areas of concern? What are outcomes that they would like to see improve or change, in both the short and long term? This evaluation of needs might include examining historical and recent data, conducting focus groups with stakeholders at various levels in the organization, and/or administering an organization-wide pre-assessment survey. From members' perspectives, where are areas that subtle bias might be at play? How do they perceive the inclusiveness of the current climate? For example, in a school context, an evaluation of data might include an analysis of student discipline and referrals, broken down by race, gender, or other demographic groups (see Appendix A for more information on how to do this). Focus groups with students, teachers, and administrators and/or a pre-assessment survey of the climate of the organization may highlight new concerns to address in the training. It is important to get multiple perspectives during this process, as each group may illuminate something unknown to the other groups.

Upon completion of the data collection, it is recommended to carefully and thoughtfully examine responses in the collaborative team (academic partners, internal members). It is helpful to then jointly identify the top three to five areas that are of concern and use those areas to focus the training. These can be good examples to use for scenarios and to integrate into the frame of the training. Ultimately, the goal of the pre-assessment stage is to have a strong understanding of what the main organization-specific topics and areas are, so that the implicit bias training can be tailored to those issues.

Content of Implicit Bias Training: What to Include?

Once the pre-planning phase is completed, the next step is developing the content of the training itself. Collaborating with academic experts is extremely helpful if the organization would like to develop and deliver the training. This content will, of course, vary depending on the context, the issues identified in the pre-implementation phase, and the instructors. Despite the need for the training to be context specific, some general structures and points can make the training successful.

Introduce the Concept of Implicit Bias

The overall flow of the training may vary, but the following pieces are likely to be important components. First, it's important to introduce the concept of implicit bias and the science behind it. While people might have heard of the term "implicit bias," often people have differing ideas of what it means. Some may mistakenly believe that it is the same as explicit, "old fashioned," racism, while others may think it is a general term that refers to any kind of prejudice or bias, regardless of level. It is important to clarify from the beginning what "implicit bias" means – unconscious associations and stereotypes about particular groups – and explain the science behind it, so that all participants have a similar understanding. Contrasting implicit bias with what it is not – it is not conscious, openly acknowledged beliefs – is also helpful in developing an understanding of this complex concept. When teaching about implicit bias and introducing the science behind it, it is helpful to keep the level of detail appropriate for the target audience (e.g., students vs. teachers vs. administrators). In any regard, describing how the brain works and functions, how it processes information (e.g., automatic vs. controlled processing), and how schemas and stereotypes are developed to provide shortcuts, often provides a foundation for understanding what implicit bias is and how it functions. (For more, see Chapters 1 and 2.)

It is also advisable to discuss where implicit bias originates. That is, why do many people hold the same implicit associations about groups, despite not explicitly endorsing these same ideas? Sources of implicit bias include the media, past experiences, and cultural exposure. This helps reinforce the point that implicit bias does not necessarily come from your own personal conscious beliefs, but rather that the broader context can create associations from repeated exposure.

Discuss When and How Implicit Bias Affects Behavior

Another important training component is addressing when and under what conditions implicit bias is most likely to affect behavior. As discussed earlier in the book, implicit bias is most likely to affect individuals' behaviors when there are time constraints, they must make quick decisions, there are a lot of stimuli around, they have little motivation to individuate people, and when the situation is ambiguous. These are the types of situations under which a person is most likely to operate under automatic processing. One of the goals of the training should be to have participants recognize when implicit bias is most likely to affect them as they perform their roles or duties, in order to better control it.

Trainings should also spend time discussing the pervasiveness of implicit bias, affecting individuals across groups, domains, and contexts. While it is also important to make training context specific, it is helpful to detail the broad reach of implicit bias across other domains, such as healthcare, policing, law, interpersonal relationships, and sports. Similarly, emphasizing that anyone, including members of stigmatized groups, can hold implicit bias due to repeated exposure to cultural stereotypes is an important point.

By first introducing how implicit bias can impact other professional organizations or domains, it eases the transition into how it might affect outcomes within the current organization or context. This funnel approach – going from broad across society to specific context – is recommended. For example, in a school-wide intervention, after discussing how implicit bias can affect police interacting with community members, doctors treating patients, and judges delivering sentences, one can turn to how it affects teachers, administrators, and fellow students in a school. A similarity between these examples is that doctors, judges, lawyers, police, and others are often motivated to be non-prejudiced, just like teachers, yet their behavior can still be affected by implicit bias. As described earlier in this book, implicit bias within a school setting might impact nonverbal behaviors, teacher–student interactions, and more subtle forms of behavior. Its impact might be seen in differential outcomes, such as discipline or suspensions. Here is where any specific data or issues within the organization that were identified in the pre-training phase should be openly discussed.

Provide Strategies to Counteract Implicit Bias

Another essential training component is strategies to counteract implicit bias (see Chapters 5 and 6). Even though it may seem impossible to remediate implicit bias, it is important to emphasize that just because someone holds implicit biases it does not mean that he or she will necessarily act in a discriminatory manner. Individual-level strategies, discussed in Chapter 5, including increased awareness, motivation to act non-prejudiced and individuate people, and engaging in controlled processing with additional time when possible, should be taught and practiced in the training. In addition, the training should teach how to change the associative structure of implicit bias in the long term – how to "rewire" these implicit stereotypes. These strategies include exposure to counter-stereotypes and increased contact with outgroup members to help counteract cultural stereotype exposure. Importantly, this is also where the larger organizational plan should be highlighted. Going beyond these individual-level strategies, what is the organization doing as a whole to promote a non-biased workplace and environment? It is also helpful to describe how this training is one piece in a larger plan, and how it connects to other initiatives and trainings, both past and present. This helps to situate the training in a broader context within the organization, and reinforces its integration into the organization's goals and future activities, rather than being a one-off training.

Integrate Implicit Bias Measurement

The Implicit Association Test (IAT) is an important tool to help measure and explain implicit bias, and is also a key strategy to incorporate into an implicit bias training (for more on the IAT, see Chapter 2). There are a few ways that one can integrate the IAT into a training, each with their strengths and benefits. Having participants in the training take the IAT using online demonstrations through Project Implicit (www.projectimplicit.org) provides first-hand experience in exploring any hidden biases participants might unintentionally hold. Typically, a variety of IATs are available online for demonstration at Project Implicit, which allows for a diversity of topics to be examined.

There are three common ways that the IAT can be integrated into an implicit bias training. One plan is to have participants take an IAT before coming to the training. Trainers may want participants to take the same IAT and then additional ones of interest, or allow freedom to investigate whichever topics are most relevant to the organization or individuals. The benefits of this approach are that participants come into the training with some prior knowledge of implicit bias and, hopefully, some recognition that it might be relevant to them. This can increase engagement and acceptance of the topic from the start of the training. It also allows for privacy so that participants can digest and process their results in a comfortable setting. This may reduce any embarrassment or upset feelings compared to when taken in a room of their peers. However, allowing this independent exploration before the trainers can frame the topic, provide relevant context, and explain what the IAT can and cannot uncover, means that it can also be a risk.

Because of this potential downside, some trainings will introduce the IAT during the training and then have participants take an IAT while at the training. This requires technological setup so that there are computer stations available with internet access or software to run IAT demonstrations, which may or may not be possible at the training site. After participants complete the IAT, they can be brought back together to debrief the process and reiterate the appropriate messaging. Depending on class size or technological difficulties, this may add additional time to the length of the training, which can be another barrier.

A final approach to integrating the IAT into training is to introduce the IAT during the training, frame the conversation, and then leave participants with information about Project Implicit to have them take an IAT in their own time afterward. This strategy saves time during the training and has the benefits of setting up the IAT, but does not allow for debriefing. Which strategy works best for an organization doing implicit bias training will depend on factors such as time allotted, resources available, and the readiness of the participants and organization. Regardless of how it is introduced, including the IAT is a valuable training tool and should be included in some format in the training.

Along with its introduction and implementation in the training, it is also important to discuss the established science and validity of the IAT, so that participants can be sure to understand what their results mean. Particularly when receiving results that they may find challenging to their beliefs, people may become skeptical or dismissive. Clearly detailing what the IAT results mean – and do not mean – must be carefully explained to reduce defensiveness.

Prioritize Participant Engagement

Throughout the entire implicit bias training, prioritizing participant engagement helps foster learning and connection with the material. One way to accomplish this goal is through active participation during the training, such as in-depth discussions both in small groups and as a larger class. Developing scenarios that are tied to the current context is a productive strategy to create engagement. For example, in a school context with racial disparities in discipline rates, a scenario might include a racial minority student not following instructions from a teacher. The scenario can then allow the participants to discuss how implicit bias might affect responses to this scenario and model different ways of responding. This can also be a useful opportunity to practice strategies to counteract implicit bias. Scenario training can first be modeled in front of the larger group, and then practiced in small groups or with partners to engage all participants.

Participant Reactions

While these suggestions can help an implicit bias training be both effective and absorbed, even the best-developed implicit bias training can have potential pushback from participants. One potential issue that might be encountered is defensiveness. That is, participants may feel that they are being "attacked" or called "racist." Reiterating that implicit bias is not the same as traditional forms of racism or bias, which are marked by their explicit belief, endorsement, and intent, can reduce this potential feeling. The setup of the training, such as discussing how societal context can create implicit bias, how people from all different backgrounds and domains can hold implicit bias, and how it does not have to do with intentions, may reduce defensiveness. By highlighting the pervasiveness of implicit bias across demographics and contexts, people feel less singled out and more willing to engage.

Another potential reaction from participants is feeling that this training "doesn't apply to me" and/or "I don't need it," because they feel that they are non-prejudiced people. This type of reaction is likely from individuals who truly believe they are egalitarian and hold that identity is central to their self-concept. To respond to these comments, it is important to acknowledge and value that non-prejudiced identity. One can be explicitly, wholeheartedly non-prejudiced, but still absorb implicit stereotypes beneath conscious awareness. This is the very group that implicit bias can impact precisely because they are unaware of it and do not believe it affects them. Playing on an individual's non-prejudiced identity can help gain buy-in to counteract more hidden biases they may hold; it provides the motivation that is essential to changing implicit biases in the long term. Emphasizing their explicit non-prejudiced beliefs as a strength in counteracting implicit bias is a key way to engage this group in the training.

Finally, another potential reaction that can arise is that a person mistakenly interprets that implicit bias is "normal" and therefore not a problem. While it is true that our brain has evolved to use shortcuts and heuristics to make quick decisions with limited cognitive capacity, it does not mean that these biases are right or unavoidable. It also does not mean that there is nothing to do about them, as they can, in fact, be countered. It is important to emphasize bias reduction strategies throughout the training, so that people are not left with the incorrect interpretation that biases are inevitable or immutable. Trainers should carefully disaffirm this belief and focus on ways to reduce the influence of implicit bias on decision-making. While other reactions and responses may arise in any training, it is important to be clear in the material being delivered, how it can apply, and what can be done about this societal problem.

Post Implicit Bias Training: The Need to Follow Up

Once training is completed, post training follow-up and assessment is important. Evaluating the training in both the short and long term is a necessary activity that is often ignored or overlooked in trainings. Immediately at the conclusion of training, evaluation might include attitudinal measures of bias, measuring learning objectives from the training, participants' motivation to counteract bias, and/or satisfaction with the training. While the immediate feedback helps gauge initial training reactions, long-term evaluations and outcome tracking can also monitor effectiveness. This is a difficult task, as it is not easy to measure implicit bias directly within an organization. Implicit bias reduction should yield changes in inequality markers of important indexes (e.g., discipline rates in schools), which might be the best or most meaningful indicator of success. Climate surveys may also track changes in attitudes and behaviors at the school or organizational level. The same data that was collected and evaluated in the pre-assessment phase should be looked at post training, and at regular intervals (three months, six months, one year, etc.). The key part is that these are long-term, ongoing processes that should be monitored.

Training as the First Step

As discussed earlier in the chapter and reiterated now due to its importance, for an intervention to be successful, implicit bias training must be part of a long-term strategy aimed at reducing bias. It is not sufficient by itself, in a vacuum, to reduce implicit bias. Having an implicit bias training in isolation can produce a "check the box" mentality that can harm progress. The larger strategy should focus on individual-level intervention, organization-wide policy change, and practice evaluation, going across multiple levels. Subsequent trainings should continue to discuss implicit bias and build on the initial foundation laid, as repeated exposure to content will help reinforce ideas and signal a longer-term commitment from the organization. As much as possible, implicit bias should be part of a regular conversation in the organization – between teachers, administrators, supervisors, and students. Policies and practices should be viewed through an implicit bias lens as part of standard practice. This type of integration has the best chance at changing implicit bias and improving outcomes in the long term.

In sum, implicit bias trainings play an important first step in addressing implicit bias within schools and organizations. However, they cannot be done in isolation and must be paired with an examination and change in policies and practices that can lead to unequal treatment. Counteracting this type of bias within an organization takes dedication, effort, and motivation across multiple levels. Ultimately, change needs to occur on the broader societal level to truly address these biases at the source, but working to change them within specific contexts and organizations plays a role in that overall process.

Reference

Kahn, K. B., Goff, P. A., & Glaser, J. (2016). Research and training to mitigate the effects of implicit stereotypes and masculinity threat on authority figures' interactions with adolescents and non-Whites. In R. J. Skiba, K. Mediratta, & M. K. Rausch (Eds.), *Inequality in school discipline: Research and practice to reduce disparities* (pp. 189–205). New York, NY: Palgrave Macmillan US.

Addressing Implicit Bias District-Wide

Experiences and Lessons Learned

Kimberly Brazwell

Introduction

For two years, I served as the director of student and community engagement for a high-performing, predominantly White and upper middle-class school district in the Midwest region of the United States. In previous years, this school district's student body included little to no racial diversity, sometimes for decades of stretches at a time. In the early 2000s, as increasing discussion developed on the social-emotional wellness and needs of students, parents within the district rated students' social and emotional health as a top priority for its schools. The superintendent understood that though the district was academically high performing, students were experiencing non-academic barriers to success – including racial inequities – preventing the critically important social-emotional wellness that parents prioritized.

School climate and community engagement work began with its International/Multicultural Education Program as a recommendation of a community task force in 1990. A steering committee comprised of faculty members from a neighboring small private liberal arts college, the school district's educators and administrators, and community members developed a definition and a mission statement for the program. To facilitate the development of the program in grades K-12, a half-time coordinator position was created. By the early 2000s, funds were allocated by the district to better support initiatives for social-emotional and multicultural programs and professional development. By 2010, the district began using commercially available tools including surveys to assess risky student behavior and the Search Institute's Developmental Assets to gauge the internal and external dynamics needed to ensure students were graduating as wholly well and emotionally stable young adults.

Recognizing that part-time work, supplemental contracts, and committees were not enough of a commitment to see social-emotional advocacy for students fully realized, a full-time administrative support position for the social-emotional needs of students was recommended by the superintendent in 2012. Infancy ideas on issues to be addressed by the support position included drug/alcohol use, poverty, and cultural competency inside and outside of the classroom. A committee was assembled and began work on the design of the position over the course of two years. The position was posted, interviews conducted, and I was offered – and I accepted – the position in the summer of 2013. I joined the district as its first administrative diversity practitioner to spearhead prosocial responses to bullying, peer pressure, and economic and racial diversity within the student body. I reported directly to the superintendent and was described as the equal opposite visionary leader to the director of instruction in that my focus was on everything *outside* of the classroom but was not designed to be direct service. Funding for the position was sourced from the district's education foundation and set-aside funds for school climate programming initiatives.

The "Right" Time and Place

Prior to transitioning into the high-performing, predominantly White and upper-middle-class school district, I had been a diversity practitioner in higher education for nearly ten years, working as the manager of diversity initiatives for the city's large, urban community during the last five years. While I loved the work and my students, I felt I would grow stagnant in the position and was looking for a new opportunity that would stretch me. Most of my work in the field involved event and program coordination as well as department management. Having solidified my skill set in diversity program coordination, I was intrigued by the idea of blending diversity and inclusion work with mental health and substance abuse prevention, intervention, and recovery. My charge in the new K-12 position was to lead efforts of school climate and community engagement. I was responsible for addressing all non-academic, social-emotional issues of students within the district and creating learning environments where school district members – both adults and students – highly valued caring for themselves, each other, and the shared community.

As a long-time advocate in the mental health community due to close family members who lived with mental health and mood disorder diagnoses, I felt like this opportunity was the right place at the right time for me to get into root cause work. Race and class are always some of the most difficult systems to tackle and I knew that working in a predominately White, wealthy community would stretch me in new ways where using empathy to do social justice work for communities that did *not* necessarily look like me would be common. My desire was to foster and support an entire community where students could be whole, authentic, and live and learn without fear while in a safe environment. I knew my plan was arguably altruistic, but I set high goals based on what I perceived to be challenging work with a ready audience.

Defining the Role

Per the language from my job description, the charge of the Office of School Climate and Community Engagement was: "to promote and enhance the overall academic mission of the school district by providing services to strengthen home, school, and community partnerships." My general goal was to address barriers to student achievement and success, and I was encouraged to build and utilize a support team who would serve together as catalysts in the development of a safe, welcoming, and sustainably inclusive learning environment. The team's objectives were to advance understanding of the emotional and social development of children and the influences of family, community, and cultural differences on student success. I was very fortunate to have a good relationship with my direct supervisor, the superintendent. Through multiple conversations, we decided to select S.M.A.R.T. (specific, measurable, achievable, relevant and timely) goals for me for the purposes of documentation. That way, the historical precedent on never-before-done position objectives could be set to show how we created and executed the groundwork.

Too Many Cooks

One of the great challenges with this position was that it had taken two years and a tremendous amount of input from community residents and district "VIPs" to create. What I believed to be my dream job on paper created a great disservice for me due to "too many cooks in the kitchen." There were too many opinions, stakeholders, and people who viewed themselves to be in positions of power and have a say in the position's design. The position was designed to cover three areas: (1) diversity, equity, and inclusion, (2) mental health, and (3) substance abuse prevention, intervention, and recovery. In layman's terms, my job was to end implicit bias, break the stigma of mental illness, and interrupt substance abuse within school district households. What could (and likely should) have been three separately staffed positions ended up being a plethora of heavy skillsets blended into one "super hero" position.

The truth is that the definition of success in my role depended on who you asked. To one success might mean: the practical application of policies, practices, and procedures of evidence-based cultural competence. Another might define success as: a provision to students of equitable access and resources to mental health and behavioral healthcare providers. A third could see success as: the institutionalization and operationalization of a restorative justice-focused drug and alcohol prevention program at all levels of the school district. Each could have consumed the time of an entire education professional! I was expected to achieve all three interpretations of success *all* within the tenure of my two-year contract.

Laying the Groundwork

Year one was all about data gathering and having as many conversations with as many people as possible. I knew the work would require the community to trust me with their most fragile personal facts and feelings, so I invested a

As discussed in Chapter 6, relationship building was a big part of the process to achieve more equity in this district. Notice here how the relationships stem from various stakeholders and work to set the stage for program development similar to the learning labs seen in Culturally Relevant Positive Behavior Interventions and Supports.

great deal of time and energy into **relationship building**. There were many powerful stakeholders and relationship brokers inside the school district who expressed interest in wanting to talk to me first. This included conversations with parents, the district's African American high school student leaders, community members, and meetings with former community residents who believed it was important for me to understand the unwritten culture of the community. Outside the school community, there were influencers and potential resource providers whose wisdom I sought for the work ahead.

With the help of the superintendent and other members of the central office administrative team, I did dig deep into the pre-existing data specific to the district. I worked closely with the identified "data folks" in the district to request and review **disaggregated data**, including the data from the PAUS student survey, Search Institute's Developmental Assets, guidance counselors, school nurses, academic intervention team, an informational interview with the director of the community's historical society, combing through high school yearbooks from throughout the 20th century, and finally my "100 conversations" with a wide range of community stakeholders. Additional data included but was not limited to school climate committee reports, funded grant projects and programs, and student engagement studies.

Like we targeted in Chapter 6 and Appendix A, data is important for guiding all interventions because it reveals problems and allows us to see whether progress is being made. Remember that disaggregated data refers to data broken down into subgroups such as by race, socioeconomic status, and gender. The data collected here is both qualitative (word-based) and quantitative (number-based), allowing for a complete understanding of the school status.

Based on a wealth of information gained from these many resources, I needed context for the quantitative data. After reviewing existing information, a research mentor suggested I get to the "origin point" of the risky behaviors and social-emotional breakdowns. I worked with a team of trusted teachers, guidance counselors, and school leaders to conduct an in-house focus group study with middle school students. Our goal was to gather qualitative data from true lived experiences of students and better understand their social-emotional needs.

I was inundated and overwhelmed with all the data. In all three areas where I was charged to develop a prosocial response, data showed that the district was not nearly as *arrived and advanced* in its current state of social-emotional wellness as hoped. Some of the more interesting discoveries follow:

Community

- Predominantly White and upper middle class
- Median income: ~$100,000
- Nearly 90% White (Projected decrease of 9% by 2060 per US Census)
  - > 25% of non-White families were economically disadvantaged
- At least 13 families experienced recent, extreme trauma (e.g., abuse, hunger, homelessness, etc.)

The Students

- 10% Culturally Diverse
  - 54% of diverse students were economically disadvantaged
  - Nearly 90% in extra- or co-curricular activities
    - After removing sports, only 18% of involved students were Culturally Diverse
- Only 50% believed they could resist drugs, alcohol and sex
- Developmental Assets
  - Significant differences between White and Culturally Diverse students
  - As compared to White students, Culturally Diverse students scored:
    - Higher in "equity and social justice" (one of few areas)
    - Lower in "peaceful conflict resolution"
- Program Enrollment
  - Over 200 students had an individualized education plan (IEP)
    - About 25% of IEPs for Culturally Diverse students
  - 11% of Culturally Diverse students took AP-level courses

Employees

- 5% Culturally Diverse.
  - Half of these employees were custodial staff
  - Only two people of Color in central office leadership team
    - Both biracial (including myself)
  - Only two Culturally Diverse teachers at secondary level

Responding to the Data

Community Town Halls for Race Dialogue

I decided to begin infrastructure-building for school climate and community engagement by creating opportunities to demonstrate and practice prosocial community dialogue. The Ohio State University's Kirwan Institute for the Study of Race and Ethnicity publishes an annual *State of the Science: Implicit Bias Review*, with one section of the 2013 report including research on implicit bias in education (Staats & Patton, 2013). I scoured this report with special attention given to the education section to gain tools on how to approach debiasing work, which I incorporated into the design of community town halls.

The Kirwan Institute for the Study of Race and Ethnicity offers high-quality research and publications on topics related to social justice and offers an acute focus on implicit bias in much of their work. Their mission is: "to create a just and inclusive society where all people and communities have opportunity to succeed" (Kirwan Institute, 2018). You can find annual *State of the Science: Implicit Bias Review* reports and detailed instructional guides for best practices with implicit bias on their website at: http://kirwaninstitute.osu.edu.

The town halls were established to increase opportunities for district residents to communicate about issues of race, ethnicity, and class identity across a spectrum of ages, races, and district roles. In the first year of my contract with the school district, three town hall sessions served as a way for the district and its residents to get to know me and to better know each other. The sessions, organized using the Art of Hosting world café format, had attendees respond to questions in small groups. I used my skill set as a visual practitioner to harvest responses from attendees and create a graphic recording of the conversations resulting in three murals that serve as artifacts of the dialogue sessions. Table 9.1 details the first year of town hall sessions.

Town halls were continued into the second academic year of my two-year contract. The pulse of the nation, including what would become the birth of the Black Lives Matter movement, seemed to prompt a call to action

Table 9.1 Year One Town Hall Sessions

Town Hall Session	Prompts	Findings
1: Cultural Code Switching	1. Adding fuel to your fire 2. Who you are culturally at home 3. "Selling out vs. keepin' it real" (honest dialogue)	Contingent on community members cautions/ concern about public conversation on race. Small turnout.
2: Multiple Identities and Blended Families	1. Our lenses 2. My people 3. Family initiation 4. Ways we form family	Better attended. Included parents and students from elementary and middle schools. Transracial adoptee families have a small but visible and vocal presence in the district's racial demographics.
3: Myth-Busting and Breaking Stereotypes	1. What parts of your identity are "awake" for this conversation? 2. How or why have you been misunderstood, misinterpreted, and misrepresented based on your identity? 3. What are you curious to understand about others' identities? 4. How do you really want others to perceive and receive your identity affinity group(s)?	Better attended. Core group established who welcomed being engaged and pushed in identity dialogue.

for us as a school community. The next town hall topic, following the death of Michael Brown, was titled, "Could Ferguson Happen in Columbus?" Because of the edgy nature of the topic, the superintendent and I worked very carefully to design the logistics of the session. We met, prior to the event, with the town mayor and chief of police to personally invite them to be present during the session. We also encouraged district central office leadership to attend, though by this point, some were beginning to have polarizing opinions about my approach to diversity and inclusion.

While all the town halls were advertised and open to the public – including community members outside of the school district – this session attracted a larger audience. One of the reasons why I was told this event was so well attended, particularly by people of Color, is that this predominantly White and wealthy community had a reputation for being perceived as unfriendly and unwelcoming to people of Color. Folks were "surprised" that *we* were having a conversation about Ferguson. Attendees were asked to think, reflect, and respond to three prompts:

1. Is the possibility of "Ferguson" in this city fact or fiction?
2. What things make you feel threatened?
3. How would total safety and security look and feel?

With the diversity of demographics and thought in the room, the session was intense and as stated by many, "emotionally exhausting." Following the town hall, a recording by mural was placed in a high-traffic hallway of the high school to passively engage students in thought and conversation.

There were three more town halls following the Ferguson Town Hall, with most responding to school culture and climate issues. For example, in response to student complaints about offensive language and terminology a "Words Hurt" educational campaign and town hall took place. Later that year, I was asked to facilitate three closed dialogue sessions with specific groups: (1) elementary school students discussing diversity, (2) a middle school class discussing race diversity and differences, and (3) a closed town hall discussing mental illness offered in conjunction with a partnership non-profit program. All were well attended due to the controlled participants and targeted, invited audiences.

The final open town hall offered was "A Critical Analysis of the Black Lives Matter Movement." By this point in my contract, I was experiencing a great deal of conflict between many community stakeholders who did not approve of my approach toward diversity and inclusion work. When the Black Lives Matter Town Hall was advertised to teaching staff, I received strong pushback from their administrative leadership about my agenda and the nature of the planned conversation. The session was decently attended, but mostly by people of Color with few, if any, White administrators or teachers in attendance. I was later told that some teachers feared I had invited political or militant radicals to the town hall. A few shared the opinion that the safety of White teachers might have been at risk if they were to have attended. Though the event was a success in attendance, I was discouraged and felt it was a missed opportunity for cross-racial dialogue among the community's White and Black residents on issues that mattered greatly for the Black community.

Continuing the Growth

During year two of my contract, I again leaned on results and lessons learned from the data gathered the previous year to design and deliver targeted professional development opportunities for the district employees offered through three initiatives:

1. A customized diversity learning community
2. A storyboard-facilitated dialogue session during a staff in-service day focused on implicit bias in the classroom
3. A one-hour professional development session with teachers in preparation for a school screening of the documentary, *I'm Not Racist, Am I?*

Pono: *A Diversity Learning Community*

Pono is a Hawaiian word that refers to the feeling that everything is all right and that someone is connected, or at one, with everything around them (Rios, 2000). The *Pono* Learning Community was designed to provide a space for open dialogue on diversity and social responsibility issues. This multi-level learning community was purposed to improve understanding of diversity topics and provide a platform for collaboration between faculty, staff, administrators, and students. Learning in the *Pono* Learning Community focused on establishing a sense of community and civic responsibility, building effective communication skills, and developing a higher capacity for critical thinking. The learning objectives of the communities stated that members would:

1. Have a greater understanding of self and the world around them;
2. Reduce fear and misunderstanding of others whose identities were different than their own;

Table 9.2 Cohort Session Identity Lenses

Faculty Cohort	Administrator Cohort
Onboarding Session	Onboarding Session
Race and Ethnicity	Sexual Orientation
Sexual Orientation	Race and Ethnicity
Religion and Faith	Intersectionality of LGBT and Gender
Class and Economic Disadvantage	Identity
Mental and Physical Health	Celebratory Reception
Power, Control, and Bullying	
Age and Generation	

3. Improve in their ability to actively participate in diverse discussions;

4. Develop an openness to others' beliefs and views;

5. Improve in their ability to dissolve misconceptions about culture.

The *Pono* Learning Community operated in cohorts with one for educators and another for administrators. From August 2014 to May 2015 the communities met monthly for two hours to reflect on different identity lenses as shown in Table 9.2.

Facilitated Dialogue Session on Implicit Bias

I had the opportunity to design a full day of professional development solely focused on non-academic barriers to success for students. The day was broken into three focal points, per the areas where district data indicated our greatest social/emotional concerns existed: (1) empathy and compassion, (2) mental health, and (3) racial implicit bias. For the racial implicit bias session, I designed an interactive presentation entitled, "Blind Spots as Barriers: When You Can't Check It at the Door." The session was held in one of the school libraries, giving teachers access to computers to first visit the Harvard University Project Implicit website (https://implicit. harvard.edu/implicit/takeatest.html) to take the racial Implicit Association Test. Following completion of the assessment, I led them through a storyboarding session where teachers were given the following prompts, which were recorded and are highlighted in Table 9.3:

Table 9.3 Selected Responses to Prompts

Classroom Diversity	Identity/Lens	Likely to Learn	More Exposure	Parking Lot
Intelligence	Diverse family members	Openness in topics	Muslim students and Islam	"I had to be right"
Desegregation and bussing	Low income	Safe space	Gender lens	Labels
Poverty inside an affluent community	First-generation college grad	International perspective	Feelings	Language and fear
OJ Simpson	Sibling/relative shadow existence	Confidence functioning in White/international environments as person of Color	Urban environments	"I don't want to say what I feel"
Rodney King	Addiction, recovery, and suicide exposure	What are the real rules?	Race diversity	Fear of bias
Haves and have nots	Dis/ability	"Protecting your brand"	Trauma	The unknown; "I don't know how to fix their problems"
National origin	Bullied experiences	Thinly veiled intolerance for the haves	Mental illness	Resiliency
Drug use	Under/overachiever	"Math doesn't judge"	Power and social status access	Bubbling tension under the lid
Free lunch or not	Divorce lens	Risk-taking	LGBT culture	What's the next revolution?
White flight	Representing your whole reference group	Intersectional beliefs and practices	Poverty	Failure happens all the time
Rural; unknowingly poor	Mental illness	Curiosity; question everything	Youth lexicon	Language and safe space
First generation	Caregiving	Peace-keeping	New silent-generation culture	Exclusion based on…
Race riots in school	Faith/religion lens	Survivor attitude	Cultural academic expectations	"What am I allowed to say?"
Religion	Southernness		Drugs and alcohol	FEAR AS A SILENCER
No conversations on diversity	Humor		Autism	
No race diversity	Personal family values		Jewish culture	
Tracking by ability			African American community	
LGBT invisible			Suburban school district pedigree	

- When I was a student, diversity in my classrooms looked like…
- An identity, lens or life experience I think I bring to the classroom is…
- Based on my lens/identity, my students likely learn…
- I admit that I could benefit from more exposure to…

During the session, participants were provided with the following resources on how a richly diverse school community might look:

- The four layers of diversity (Loden, & Rosener, 1991):
    - Individual Dimensions: self (including personality type, communication styles, conflict management styles, learning styles, etc.)
    - Internal Dimensions: race, age, gender identity, sexual orientation, ability/able-bodiness, nationality/ethnicity, and immigration status
    - External Dimensions: geographic location, socioeconomic status, personal habits, hobbies/spare time activities, religion/spirituality, education, experience, appearance/size, parental status, and marital status
    - Organizational Dimensions: functional level/classification, work content/field, seniority, division/department/unit/group, work location, union affiliation, and management status
- The six emotions with which humans are naturally wired:
    - Happiness
    - Anger
    - Sadness
    - Disgust
    - Embarrassment
    - Surprise
- A diagram showing the intersectionality of values, beliefs, expectations, attitudes, and actions
- A handout created by social justice filmmaker and practitioner, Lee Mun Wah, entitled: "21 Ways to Stop a Conversation About Diversity"

Training Session for Film Screening

I'm Not Racist… Am I? is a documentary about 12 teenagers from New York City who spent one school year talking about race and privilege in a series of workshops and in conversations with friends and family members. The film screenings were scheduled as a middle school assembly, high school assembly, and evening public screening. In preparation for the highly sensitive racial content of the documentary, teachers were provided with an hour-long professional development to prepare them for potential student dialogue and engagement on race after the screening of the film.

The hour-long session with secondary teachers consisted of the following:

1. Review of "Unpacking the Invisible Knapsack" by Peggy McIntosh (1988).
   a. Educators sat in pairs and shared personal stories prompted by one of the examples from McIntosh's list.
2. Exploration of the "Privilege of Numbness" article by Lee Mun Wah (2013).
3. Discussion and reflection on my experiences talking with students who would only share stories of marginalization in a one-on-one setting and why that occurs.
4. Viewing of the TEDtalk: "Color Blind or Color Brave" (Hobson, 2014).

The discussion focused on how the presence of different identity lenses meant a presence of different realities, which often fuels instances of benefiting from the privilege of not experiencing others' pain. To prepare teachers for various visible and invisible film reactions (including their own), we continued work on managing and improving our own implicit biases to better support students with empathy and compassion. Key factors in our preparation for student support were:

1. Developing the curiosity to know what students' stories and perspectives were;
2. Ensuring we provided safe spaces for students to learn and exist;
3. Exhibiting an ability to affirm student stories once they were comfortable talking with us.

Because the documentary was not available outside of the public screening, a letter including links to the film's website, where the film's content was detailed, was sent to every middle and high school student's household along with a waiver allowing parents to decide to opt their student out of attending the school screening. Parents and community members were welcomed and encouraged to attend the screening of the film. As an added opportunity for enriched dialogue, the film director, Catherine Wigginton Greene, was present for the screenings and follow-up conversations. Guests were encouraged to engage the director in conversation, especially after the evening screening where there was a longer duration of time scheduled to talk and reflect.

The film screenings of *I'm Not Racist... Am I?* did much more than create school dialogue on the topic of racial implicit bias; they created an explosion of emotion. Screenings for the middle and high schools played to auditoriums packed with nearly entire student bodies. Following the school screenings, several students and families of Color shared privately that they felt affirmed by the documentary. However, many White students were greatly offended by the film's perceived accusation of posturing Whites as being racist and shared their displeasure with their parents. The public screening later that evening was poorly attended with a mere 70 people in a 400-seat auditorium and subsequent discussion that was raw, defensive, and hostile. I received disturbing emails following the screening that detailed anger rippling through White homes in the school community. Due to the controversy, some of my administrative colleagues were not comfortable engaging students and teachers in race dialogue during the days and weeks subsequent to the film screenings. It was explained that teachers did not feel adequately prepared to facilitate conversations about race with students. A few teachers, whose students organically began discussing the film, redirected conversation. I was told some teachers were so personally disturbed that they did not feel they *could* speak about it with or in front of students. The film came and went. And we didn't talk about it directly or in detail again. *I'm Not Racist... Am I?*, in retrospect, became a defining moment between the district and me. A bold attempt at addressing racial implicit bias head-on turned into scandal for the district, physiological trauma for me, and a wound the school community and I could not seem to come together to heal.

Discoveries

Interesting patterns regarding mental illness, substance abuse, and socio-economic status existed, and not just in the district where I was employed.

When I conferred with colleagues in other wealthy suburban districts, they had data or anecdotal evidence of students with high manifestations of anxiety and depression as early as third grade. The pattern I noticed was that many students who eventually misused and abused substances also struggled with challenges that resembled (or were officially diagnosed as) mental health and mood disorders. Students learned by middle and high school to self-medicate with alcohol and drugs to cope – and had the financial means to do so.

On the other hand, the few students of low socioeconomic status who experienced issues with mental illness tended to *pop up on the radar* through teacher intervention meetings and disciplinary infractions. At one point, I consulted with a clinical counselor, who supported the school district through an alcohol, drug, and mental health grant, about the link between mental health and cultural competency. She informed me that depression is expressed differently in White girls than it is in African American girls. She explained, when White girls are depressed they are more likely to self-harm (e.g., "cut"), but when African American girls are depressed they are more likely to get into fights. Therefore, teachers are more likely to refer White female students suffering from depression to mental health resources for counseling while the African American female students are left to be suspended or expelled instead.

Achieving "Buy-In"

Perhaps one of the oddities of my experience was that the district already bought in to the *theoretical* idea that implicit bias was a *thing* – I just don't think they thought *they* exhibited implicit bias. One might even surmise that the employees and community members perceived race and economic bias as classless and uncivil rather than morally reprehensible. It seemed the notion of 'isms was perceived more as a character flaw than a personal and institutional construct requiring constant and sustainable pressure for deconstruction.

In year one of my contract, I frequently discussed systemic issues as academic barriers to student (and employee) success. However, in year two, I attempted to implement programs to positively address systemic issues. In fact, it was after my first year that I was given the opportunity to design a the previously discussed professional development day solely focusing on social-emotional issues. Even with "buy-in" from the district, I received pushback.

Challenges to My Difficult but Necessary Journey

From early on I could see that to respond to the data-driven issues, I had to touch some culture, climate, and value systems that long-time members of the school community had – consciously or unconsciously – considered "untouchable." I knew I needed to have social justice-related conversations with people who were not used to being "called out" and questioned regarding their regular diversity and inclusion efforts. I pursued conversations with governmental officials, police, and even more complicated dialogue and pressing conversations with my colleagues on the administrative team.

Some of the people who viewed themselves as allies to my social justice efforts ended up becoming potential barriers to foundation-building as we got deeper into the practice. Conversations on diversity, equity, and inclusion occurred in the past, but few to no Brown people were in the room when those conversations took place over a decade ago. In addition to standard implicit bias, I was faced with combating the guilt and discomfort of well-meaning and good-intentioned White folks who couldn't realistically see themselves as contributing in *any* way to the problem of race and class issues in the district. I spoke my mind about challenges that seemed to highlight where we fell short of the altruistic goal of "advancing understanding of the emotional and social development of children and the influences of family, community, and cultural differences on student success." However, I was surprised by my White colleagues' frustration and anger about being offered the thought that they may still have race-related biases, stereotypes, and values that needed altering. Instead of being able to see outside of themselves regarding how they might unconsciously contribute to a culture of racism and classism, the staff often perpetuated unconscious bias instead.

Rising Tensions

Over time the tension began to build and concerns for my well-being grew within my personal circles. My mother became increasingly concerned about the safety of me traveling at night to and from the school community. The community had already had a reputation – whether perceived or real – of targeting Black drivers passing through the community. Once I had upset the police department – especially the police chief – my family speculated about the possibility of the police department searching plates on my car or digging into my legal history. I never worried about those things, but overall, my safety became an increasing concern for my family. They feared the number of "enemies" I was making on the job. The person hired to be a peacemaker and a community convener for the district's school climate and community engagement had, in effect, become a polarizing figure.

Most of the folks I pushed for avoided me and most of the folks I pushed against conflicted with me. Once the tension I was experiencing had become both commonplace and traumatic, my family members frequently offered critical commentary that I was pressing "too hard" and "too fast" in trying to aid the school district in debiasing efforts. Close friends and family thought I should have paced myself and acquiesced more to those in the district community with power, privilege, and social capital.

It was my opinion, however, that the proverbial "house was on fire" and that I needed to respond to the race and class power differential with immediacy. I perceived the students of Color and students living in poverty to be in social-emotional danger. They were not holistically well and were barely "surviving" the environment. **I made the conscious decision to press firmly and boldly and to advance against anything and everything I perceived as implicit bias.** I believed I approached the debiasing efforts in a way that was challenging but fostered unique learning opportunities. In retrospect, the mere fact that I openly and pervasively challenged White privilege, class privilege, and White fragility in a predominantly White, wealthy, and power-rich community *was* the affront.

Unfound Support

One of the biggest and most impactful surprises was the reaction I received from the student community and the race minority community to my advocacy efforts. I was hoping to be able to serve as their "fearless" advocate and champion. However, I was shocked to realize that my spirited approach resulted in me being avoided by Brown students, Brown parents, and marginalized folks in general. I talked about many taboo issues head-on, which was especially rare in this predominately White and wealthy community. Most students didn't want to have anything to do with me or be seen anywhere near my office. At one point, a student told me directly that most students in the high school thought my efforts were laughable and that I was a joke. The handful of students who ingratiated themselves to me as ally students had – in many ways – already been rejected based on race and class: they had nothing to lose.

Most other students who felt like they had an opportunity to be accepted by their peers in the school district avoided me. When I passed them in hallways, they avoided making eye contact with me. Their parents rarely responded to my proactive communications, and most of the events I offered for students of Color were poorly attended at best. In some cases, I spoke with parents of Color only when their child was in disciplinary trouble and they felt forced to intervene on their child's behalf. I had many occasions when I had already received testimonials and heartbreaking stories of trauma from students, parents, and teachers regarding race, class, mental health, and substance abuse issues; when it came time for me to stand up to those in positions of power on their behalf, the "victims" were nowhere in sight.

I was completely unprepared to be unsupported by the communities who shared my affinity lenses. I am race diverse. I am a woman. I am a young leader. I was raised in poverty. I have family members with serious mental illness and mood disorders. I have family members in addiction recovery. On paper, I thought I was a perfect fit for this position. What I didn't realize was that the communities of the very people I represented had already disengaged to a certain degree from their affinity groups to receive acceptance from the predominant community. Their lack of support in voice and action rendered me "ineffective" in front of my White colleagues. To them I seemed unable to establish relationships both with people who looked like me and those who did not. Subsequently, a narrative developed that I was, perhaps, incompetent because I couldn't produce the results the district was seeking with regards to my relationship with Brown students. It was a crushing blow to my advocating heart and my confidence in my ability to build communities with great success.

If I could add support to this position, it should be actionable and united, looking like:

- "Required..." When diversity, equity and inclusion activities are offered to students, teachers and administrators as "optional," there is a high likelihood that participation will not take place or will be minimal
- Market value pay
- Vocalized support from fellow administrators in public
  - Private meetings for touch-base and clarification welcome
- Assigned administrative assistant
- Compensated/recognized student ambassadors
- Parent Resource Group Program: Development of parent support groups based on affinity (e.g., Black parents, divorced parents, LGBTQ+ parents, etc.)
- Data dashboard of Diversity and Inclusion
  - Good and bad comments from World Café publicly posted

A Dedicated Mission

If I had the ability to serve the school district in the school climate and community engagement leadership position again, I don't know that I would lead differently. I still believe that the social-emotional issues in the district were at a fever pitch and needed to be addressed head-on. I believed then – and still believe – that the root cause issues underlying the implicit race and class bias in the school community needed to be visible to give context to the real approaches imperative for authentic and sustainable debiasing work. In my personal and professional opinion, the first attempt at this job required trailblazing and the truth is that trailblazing is often thankless, messy work.

Advice for Leaders Preparing to Initiate Change

Do...

- Remember that **pacing matters**.
  - Going too fast aggravates the system and increases the likelihood that the "good work" will be rejected.

- Going too slow perpetuates the "status quo" by appearing as passive permission for the environmental members to behave as usual because "nothing's wrong."
- **Play politics** within social justice.
  - There's a saying that culture eats strategy for breakfast; it's true. Don't underestimate the power of "social capital" leaders and longstanding norms as you develop plans to usher in change and paradigm shifts. Change *is* political.
  - Find out who the school community favorites are – teachers, administrators, staff persons – and understand who favors them and why. Your support and more importantly, your advocacy, could be at stake if you "cross" the wrong person.
- Build in **strategies for self-care**.
  - A social justice leadership role might trigger past trauma or secondary trauma stemming from the emotional exhaustion of serving traumatized people.
  - The work is emotionally draining, isolating, and can take a toll on the practitioner's holistic wellness.
  - It's not uncommon for a practitioner to leave the job "sicker" than how s/he arrived.

Do Not...

- **Show your cards** right away.
  - If stakeholders know everything you're going to do, how you're going to do it, and if *any* part of your plan is perceived to be scary or intimidating, your plans can be stopped.
- **Press too hard** for too long.
  - It's one thing to bear the bad news that highly educated and well-meaning professionals might not be as "good" as anticipated. It's an entirely different story when one chooses to enforce culture and climate change by regularly holding professionals accountable to make changes that better meet the needs of racially diverse students.
  - If you perpetually make powerful people uncomfortable – especially if they're not used to being uncomfortable – you may be pressured to leave.

Structural Recommendations

- Schedule **regulated and predictable hours** for the Office of School Climate and Community Engagement.
    - This position was designed to operate at second shift to better accommodate student and family needs that might arise after school hours. Parents suggested that the district look into a more regulated and predictable schedule for the role.
- Create separate, **designated spaces** for social-emotional office work and events/programs.
    - Based on the high need for diversity and inclusion efforts to manifest warm and inviting aesthetics, an established location creates a diversity and inclusion-friendly safe space, e.g., a diversity lounge.
- Offer **mobile office spaces** due to the school-to-school travel needs of the role.
    - Allow work from various locations and "squatter" spaces throughout the district to better gauge the culture and climate of the district.
- Set aside **time for data** collection, analysis, and evaluation.
- Expand **"human" resources**.
    - When more people in the district and community understand the moral imperative of the position, efficacy is increased.
    - Add layers to the position constituency partners, including more racially diverse individuals.
        - Partners may include: student ambassadors, community representatives (e.g., police, government, faith-based organizations, businesses, schools, service nonprofits), designated employee representatives, parent teacher organizations, and parent resource groups.
        - Suggested affinity-based parent resource groups: African American, New Americans, divorced/single parents, LGBTQ+, special needs and families new to the community.
- Maintain a **parent advocacy program**.
    - Provide parents and students with a toolkit to navigate unique cultural challenges within the district.
    - Offer regularly scheduled workshops for parents that create a space where they can connect with and support each other.

- Suggested "how to" workshops:
  - Speak at a board meeting
  - Write a letter/document an incident
  - Get resources based on low income
  - Prepare for a meeting with an administrator
  - Get funding for programs
  - Understand policy
  - Access district data
  - Ask for what you want and/or need
  - Tell personal diversity and inclusion stories
- Provide formal and informal **diversity and inclusion trainings** for educators and administrators
  - Use data to determine the specific needs of district employees.
  - Equip faculty and staff with **knowledge and resources** to better understand that race, class, gender, and sexual orientation are factors in student experiences being positive or negative.
  - Suggested offerings include:
    - Arts-based diversity training
    - Diversity assessment and metrics
    - Linking curriculum to social justice
    - Implicit bias
      - Debiasing opportunities must be frequent.
    - Study Circles with *Everyday Antiracism*
- Host regularly scheduled **open dialogue sessions** for diversity and inclusion practice.
  - Allow faculty, staff, students, and parents the opportunity to de-bias in a practice of "learning by doing."
  - Suggested opportunities:
    - World Café
      - Four per year for community
      - Four per year for middle school
      - Two per year for elementary school and high school
    - School–Community Town Halls
      - Require attendees from all constituency groups.
    - Student–Teacher Learning Communities
- Make staff involved in diversity and inclusion work **highly visible** to various school district stakeholders.

- Allow for substantial **face time** with students and teachers at each school building.
  - More time will increase knowledge and learning about social-emotional and diversity and inclusion issues at each school building.
- Suggested opportunities for high visibility:
  - Professional Learning Community meetings
  - Faculty, staff, or administrator meetings
  - District-wide meetings
  - School-Community Town Halls
  - Parent resource group workshops and meetings
  - School Climate discussions
  - Counselor and mental health clinician meetings
  - Central office staff meetings
  - Curriculum planning meetings

Other Considerations

- Racism and classism, when addressed together, increase White fragility.
- People of Color in a predominantly White and wealthy community also have or benefit from class privilege.
  - May not be fast allies toward leaders of Color.
- Social capital matters!
  - Popular educators and administrators in the district have more power than positional leaders.

If Your...

- **District struggles to support Black students**
  RECOMMENDATION: programs and initiatives that intentionally and exclusively target and empower Black students
- **District struggles to support low income students**
  RECOMMENDATION: special identity PTOs trained to advocate for students with special circumstances and needs
- **District struggles to use multiple versions of fit, vision, values, lenses, and methods**

RECOMMENDATION: regularly scheduled community conversations with faculty, staff, administrators, and community stakeholders present

- **District struggles with messy process vs. clear, defined goals with an end result**
  RECOMMENDATION: regularly scheduled diversity training and diversity practice for faculty, staff, and administrators

How to Achieve...

...a warm, safe and nurturing learning environment for children and adults, characterized by an appreciation for the culture, achievements, accomplishments, challenges, and struggles of all people.

...according to minority parents in the district

- Create a **policy of advocacy**
  - Co-create (with students and teachers) a script for students to use when they feel or experience discriminatory situations.
  - Offer professional development workshops to students and teachers on the challenges students face and how to use the script.
  - Students and teachers should practice using the script to develop students' empowerment and allow teachers to see what student advocacy can look like.
- Hire **diverse** educators, administrators, and head coaching staff.
- Continue to celebrate and explore **Black History Month**.
- **Shift power** to other stakeholders (inclusively!).
- Create an environment where minority students and parents feel as **valued** as anyone else.
- Offer clear and consistent **response strategies** to create safer spaces.
- Hold the district accountable for **social-emotional wellness priorities** (to create learning environments to support the social and emotional health of its community members).
  - Commit to providing aligned development opportunities (diversity, empathy/compassion, student advocacy).
    - School board development should align for at least 50% of scheduled trainings.
    - Make professional development hours mandatory for administrators.

- Devote a portion of student time to the same topics and practices.
- Create hours where staff are required to evaluate classroom practice with evidence.
- Provide support and opportunities for all students to excel in honors and AP courses.
- Create a culture where self-advocating students are **supported** (not disciplined) by staff, faculty, and administrators.
- Teachers should be expected to **hold high expectations** of all students and **believe** that all students, regardless of race and class, are as capable and intelligent as any other student.
- Hold a **high level of sensitivity** to racial issues.
  - Flawed, incumbent value systems must be counteracted by increasing the presence of African American staff and intentionally employing those who embrace diversity.
  - Embed systems of change in schools as a cultural norm rather than a periodic event.
    - Focus change efforts in ways that mirror building best practices.
  - Foster a resulting paradigm shift as it transfers values from staff to students.
- A district embracing diversity would have:
  - More teachers that were Brown throughout all the schools.
  - Zero tolerance for ignorant, racial comments made or dismissed.
  - A minority parent council.
  - Successes with rescuing struggling minority students.

References

Hobson, L. (2014). *Color blind or color brave* [video recording]. TEDtalk. Retrieved from www.ted.com/talks/mellody_hobson_color_blind_or_color_brave?language=en

Kirwan Institute. (2018, May 9). *Kirwan Institute: About*. Retrieved from http://kirwaninstitute.osu.edu/about/#overview

Loden, M., & Rosener, J. B. (1991). *Workforce America! Managing employee diversity as a vital resource*. Homewood, IL: Business One Irwin.

McIntosh, P. (1988). Unpacking the invisible knapsack. *Peace and Freedom*, *12*. Retrieved from http://hd.ingham.org/Portals/HD/White%20 Priviledge%20Unpacking%20the%20Invisible%20Knapsack.pdf

Mun Wah, L. (2013, May). *The privilege of numbness*. Retrieved from www. stirfryseminars.com/pdfs/2013_newsletters/newsletter_may2013.pdf

Rios, C. (2000). *Ka hana pono*. [Divination cards]. Puna, HI: Connie Rios.

Staats, C., & Patton, C. (2013). *State of the Science: Implicit Bias Review 2013*. Columbus, OH: Kirwan Institute for the Study of Race and Ethnicity. Retrieved from www.kirwaninstitute.osu.edu/reports/2013/ 03_2013_SOTS-Implicit_Bias.pdf

Appendix A
DATA: Detailed, Accurate, and Tracked Awareness

It was a dark and stormy night as Principal Stanton sat at the computer with the eerie, greenish glow of the spreadsheet emanating into the dimly lit room... If this sounds like your typical Thursday night, you are not alone. For many administrators, data sounds more like a horror novel than a tool, and with the growing amount of culpability associated with "the numbers," it is not surprisingly so. Many modern school administrators have been thrown into a world of data-based decision-making with little or no training on data analysis and/or use and even less support when it comes to understanding the numbers. Fortunately, many resources exist that can help you work *with* rather than work *through* the data in ways that will support your leadership instead of hindering your progress.

The Data Cycle

A thermometer only provides meaningful data if you want to know about the temperature, if it is working correctly, and if it can relay temperature changes. When it comes to school data it is no more complicated: data must provide details about what is going on in the school, reflect accurate information, and include items that can be tracked over time. To keep data usage for inequities simple, McIntosh and colleagues (2018) break down the process into four steps:

1. Problem identification
2. Problem analysis

3. Intervention planning

4. Monitoring.

Really this process is more of a cycle where monitoring identifies new or modified problems and begins the process again, so we will call this The Data Cycle as is demonstrated in Figure A1.

Problem Identification

To begin the data cycle, schools must collect indicator data related to key outcomes by subgroup, such as how many Hispanic students are enrolled in special education courses. Alone, this is simply a number, but when paired with similar school-wide data, it becomes more informative and what statisticians refer to as descriptive. For example, you can calculate the absolute rate for special education enrollment for Hispanic students. You would do this by taking the number of Hispanic students in special education and dividing it by the total number of Hispanic students in the

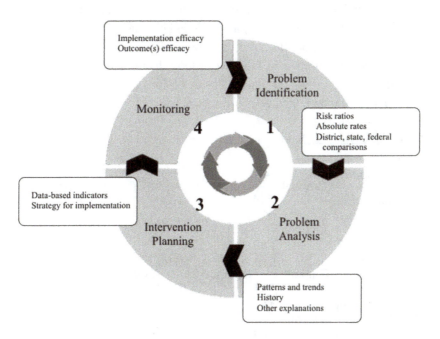

Figure A1 Visual Representation of The Data Cycle with Important Elements

189

Table A1 Raw Data for Sample Calculations

Students with...	Grade 9	Grade 10	Grade 11	Grade 12	Total
Suspension	47	58	34	12	151
Detentions	510	510	483	388	1891
Enrolled	744	1053	987	925	3709

school. In a school with Hispanic, White, and African American students, you could then repeat this calculation for White and African American students in order to have comparable percentages of students.

Another way to compare these numbers is by risk ratio. Here you divide the absolute rate for Hispanic students by the absolute rate for White students to find the likelihood that a Hispanic student is enrolled in special education versus a White student, where numbers greater than 1 mean the Hispanic student is more likely and less than 1 indicate the Hispanic student is less likely (and 1 signifying exactly the same). You can think of this as: Hispanic students are _____ times more likely to be enrolled in special education than White students. When you get a number less than 1, you can flip this to be White students are ___ times more likely than Hispanic students by dividing 1 into the previous number. You can extend this to comparison at the district-, state-, and federal levels as well. For now, let's look at some high school discipline data by grade.

From the raw numbers in Table A1, it looks like detentions are similar for grades 9–11 and less for grade 12; suspensions appear more likely in grades 9 and 10 than later grades.

First find the Absolute Rate:

$$= \frac{\#\ suspended}{\#\ enrolled} = \text{Grade 9: } \frac{47}{744}; \text{ Grade 10: } \frac{58}{1053}; \text{ Grade 11: } \frac{34}{987};$$

$$\text{Grade 12: } \frac{12}{925}; \text{ Overall: } \frac{151}{3709}$$

$$= \frac{\#\ detentions}{\#\ enrolled} = \text{Grade 9: } \frac{510}{744}; \text{ Grade 10: } \frac{510}{1053}; \text{ Grade 11: } \frac{483}{987};$$

$$\text{Grade 12: } \frac{388}{925}; \text{ Overall: } \frac{1891}{3709}$$

Table A2 Absolute Rates from Sample Calculations (in Decimal Form)

Absolute Rate of...	Grade 9	Grade 10	Grade 11	Grade 12	Overall
Suspension	.063	.055	.034	.013	.041
Detentions	.685	.484	.489	.419	.510

Table A3 Absolute Rates from Sample Calculations (in Percentage Form)

Absolute Rate of...	Grade 9	Grade 10	Grade 11	Grade 12	Overall
Suspension	6.3%	5.5%	3.4%	1.3%	4.1%
Detentions	68.5%	48.4%	48.9%	41.9%	51.0%

The absolute rates calculated (see Table A2) can also be expressed as percentages by moving the decimals two places to the right (see Table A3).

Notice that even though ninth and tenth graders had the same exact number of detentions, ninth graders are nearly a full percent higher. It looks like ninth graders are being disciplined more than the other students, whereas twelfth graders are not being suspended often. Differences show 17.5 percentage points more ninth graders getting detentions, and 2.3 more percentage points getting more suspensions than the typical high school students, making it seem like detentions are a big deal. Let's see how much of a difference there *really* is between these groups and the general school population.

Now find the risk ratio

$$= \frac{\text{Abs rate Grade 9}}{\text{Abs rate Overall}} = \text{Suspension: } \frac{.063}{.041} = 1.5; \text{ Detention: } \frac{.685}{.510} = 1.3$$

$$= \frac{\text{Abs rate Grade 12}}{\text{Abs rate overall}} = \text{Suspension: } \frac{.013}{.041} = .317$$

$$(\text{inverse/flipped} = \frac{1}{.317} = 3.2)$$

Ninth graders are 1.5 times (or 50%) more likely to get suspended, and 1.3 times (or 30%) more likely to get a detention than the average high school student. A twelfth grader is about one-third (32%) less likely to get suspended than the average high school student. Stated differently, the average high school student is 3.2 times (320%) more likely than a twelfth grader to get suspended. Considering these rates, it seems like the biggest problems are ninth graders being over-suspended and twelfth graders being under-suspended. We can even compare these two critical groups.

$$\frac{Abs\ rate\ Grade\ 9}{Abs\ rate\ Grade\ 12} = \frac{.063}{.013} = 4.8$$

Ninth graders are 4.8 times more likely to be suspended than twelfth graders.

Using descriptive statistics to compare our group representation takes the data much further and clarifies the picture of what is occurring. While ageism is not the typical culprit of implicit bias in high schools, data can be broken down by any subgroup: race, ethnicity, socioeconomic status, gender, special education enrollment, etc. You may even want to look at the data for under-representation in programs such as Advanced Placement, extracurriculars, sports, and gifted and talented programs.

Problem Analysis

The next step is to take the identified problem areas and look for patterns and trends. Some schools have data organization software such as the School-Wide Information System (see www.pbisapps.org) or PowerSchool (see www.powerschool.com) that display data by specific criteria such as discipline by time of day, behavior type, or incident location; or academics by teacher, home location, and extracurricular involvement. This kind of analysis might simply involve looking at numbers and graphs or can be as complicated as having a member of your data team perform high-level statistical modeling. Regardless, at this point you identify areas where inequities tend to emerge. Maybe students who play sports are more likely to experience differences by race in special education enrollment, or low socioeconomic students have greater gender differences in detention rates. Data can also be analyzed in comparison to previous data, such as by considering differences between student test scores in elementary and high school or before and after an intervention. It's important not to assume you know why these relationships exist, but to consider a wide variety of explanations instead. This will allow you to identify problems of note and create the most constructive interventions that are focused on data rather than assumptions.

Intervention Planning

While this is a critical step of the data cycle, intervention planning's intricacies are beyond the scope of this book. For discipline, systems such as Restorative Practices and Positive Behavior Interventions and Supports are popular and shown to reduce exclusionary discipline overall (Vincent & Tobin, 2010) and in culturally relevant cases, reduce racial discipline gaps (Bal, 2018; Bal, Kozleski, & Thorius, 2012; Gregory, Clawson, Davis, & Gerewitz, 2015; Vincent, Inglish, Girvan, Sprauge, & McCabe, 2016; Vincent, Randall, Cartledge, Tobin, & Swain-Bradley, 2011). Academic systems such as Response-to-Intervention have been successful at lessening achievement gaps as well but need to be monitored regularly for consistency (Alonzo, Tindel, & Robinson, 2008). Meanwhile, researchers suggest that links between academics and discipline allow for interventions in either to benefit the other (Gregory, Skiba, & Noguera, 2010). Furthermore, implicit bias-focused efforts might reflect a professional development-enrooted approach as discussed in Chapters 6 and 8. As long as you have a plan, you will need indicators to measure the efficacy and integrity and a separate plan on how to implement that intervention plan. Planning is key.

Monitoring

While monitoring will look different depending on your specific needs and interventions, you must remember to include three key elements in your assessment: (1) plan implementation integrity, (2) plan efficacy indicators, and (3) standard identifiers. The first element ensures that your intervention is actually happening and involves observing faculty and staff to make sure there is consistent implementation. Efficacy indicators will be driven by your findings in problem analysis and actual intervention plan, but standard identifiers remain static. In other words, if you find that students of Color are not enrolling in extracurricular activities, your change in enrollment would show if your plan is effective; meanwhile, you will still look at test scores and graduation rates as standard indicators of student success.

We hope this appendix provided you with a tool to begin using data in your school, but recognize there is much more to learn. For a more detailed guide on using data for school discipline equity, visit https://files.eric.ed.gov/fulltext/ED573680.pdf. This report, *School Discipline Data Indicators: A Guide for Districts and Schools*, offers step-by-step instructions for data use inclusive of statistical explanations and resources for further assistance (Nishioka, Shigeoka, & Lolich, 2017). While this report focuses on school discipline, most of the content can be applied to academic data as well.

References

Alonzo, J., Tindal, G., & Robinson, Q. (2008). Using schoolwide response to intervention to close the achievement gap in reading. *ERS Spectrum, 26*(1), 1–9.

Bal, A. (2018). Culturally responsive positive behavioral interventions and supports: A process-oriented framework for systemic transformation. *Review of Education, Pedagogy, and Cultural Studies, 40*(2), 144–174. https://doi.org/10.1080/10714413.2017.1417579

Bal, A., Kozleski, E., & Thorius, K. K. (2012). *Culturally relevant positive behavior support matters* (Equity Matters: In Learning, for Life). Tempe, AZ: The Equity Alliance at Arizona State University. Retrieved from www.equityallianceatasu.org/sites/default/files/CRPBIS_Matters.pdf

Gregory, A., Clawson, K., Davis, A., & Gerewitz, J. (2015). The promise of Restorative Practices to transform teacher-student relationships and achieve equity in school discipline. *Journal of Educational and Psychological Consultation, 25*, 1–29.

Gregory, A., Skiba, R. J., & Noguera, P. A. (2010). The achievement gap and the discipline gap: Two sides of the same coin? *Educational Researcher, 39*(1), 59–68.

McIntosh, K., Ellwood, K., McCall, L., & Girvan, E. J. (2018). Using discipline data to enhance equity in school discipline. *Intervention in School and Clinic, 53*(3), 146–152.

Nishioka, V., Shigeoka, S., & Lolich, E. (2017). *School discipline data indicators: A guide for districts and schools* (No. REL 2017–240). Washington, DC: U.S. Department of Education, Institute of Education Sciences, National Center for Education Evaluation and Regional Assistance, Regional Educational Laboratory Northwest.

Vincent, C. G., & Tobin, T. (2010). The relationship between implementation of school-wide positive behavior support (SWPBS) and disciplinary exclusion of students from various ethnic backgrounds with and without disabilities. *Journal of Emotional and Behavioral Disorders, 19*(4), 217–232.

Vincent, C. G., Inglish, J., Girvan, E. J., Sprague, J. R., & McCabe, T. M. (2016). School-wide positive and restorative discipline (SWPRD): Integrating school-wide positive behavior interventions and supports and restorative discipline. In R. J. Skiba, K. Mediratta, & M. K. Rausch (Eds.), *Inequality in school discipline* (pp. 115–134). New York, NY: Palgrave Macmillan US.

Vincent, C. G., Randall, C., Cartledge, G., Tobin, T., & Swain-Bradley, J. (2011). Toward a conceptual integration of cultural responsiveness and schoolwide positive behavior support. *Journal of Positive Behavior Interventions, 13*(4), 219–229.